Winter Past:
The Spirit of Hope

John O'Brien OFM

© John O'Brien OFM 2024

Other books by the author

Catch the Wind
Return to Gethsemane
My one Friend is Darkness
Rachel's Tears and Mary's Song
Love Rescue Me
Cry Me a River
Therese and the Little Way of Love and Healing
Clare of Assisi: A living Flame of Love
Waiting for God: From Trauma to Healing
With Thee Tender is the Night
Loneliness Knows My Name
Silent Music of Love: Teach Us to Pray
A Love Supreme
At Eternity's Gate: Artists of the Infinite
The Darkness Shall be the Light: T.S. Eliot's Journey to Faith
The Crucible of Doubt: Dostoevsky's Faith
The Outsiders: God's Lonely People

To
The Breakfast Club Multyfarnham,
Fiona, Jack and Ciara Oliver,
Seán and Marci MacNamara,
Bill and Mary Gibbons

R.I.P.
Greig Oliver,
Ria and Carlo Quintilliani

"The birds they sang
At the break of day
Start again
I heard them say
Don't dwell on what
Has passed away
Or what is yet to be.
Ah the wars they will
Be fought again
The holy dove
She will be caught again
Bought and sold
And bought again
The dove is never free.
Ring the bells that still can ring
Forget your perfect offering
There is a crack a crack in everything
That's how the light gets in."

(Anthem – Leonard Cohen)

"See! The winter is past;
the rains are over and gone.
Flowers appear on the earth;
the season of singing has come,
the cooing of doves
is heard in our land.
The fig tree forms its early fruit;
the blossoming vines spread their fragrance.
Arise, come, my darling;
my beautiful one, come with me."

(Song of Songs 2:11-13)

Contents

Introduction 7

Chapter 1 Seeking 10

Chapter 2 All is Grace 28

Chapter 3 Where is Love? 63

Chapter 4 The Spirituality of Paul the Apostle 86

Chapter 5 Into the Desert 99

Chapter 6 Prayer of Abandonment 115

Chapter 7 Dance Me to the End of Love 128

Introduction

Andy Warhol (+1987), birth name Andrew Warhola, was an American visual artist, film director and leading figure in the pop art movement. Some of his best known works are the paintings "Campbell's Soup Cans" (1962) and the "Marilyn Diptych" (1962). He was born in Pittsburgh in 1928. Andy was born Andy Warhola and belonged to the John Chrysostom Byzantine Catholic Church (Byzantine-Rutherian rite) a church that is in full communion with the Roman Catholic Church. He would have been familiar with the world of icons. Warhol went to Mass here with his mother, Julia. She lived with Andy for two decades after he came to New York. She prayed each day with him before he left for work. As a young man in Pittsburgh he often went to four lengthy services over a weekend, and spent a lot of time staring at religious icons. Later as an adult in New York he would stop in daily at St. Vincent Ferrer parish church on the Upper East Side of Manhattan. He would often be seen going into the church at midday to light a candle and spending some quiet time in prayer. This would have influenced him in looking at what our modern icons are. His images of consumerism and violence show us what we have become used to. His violent images such as the electric chair and a car crash reflect to us what we take for granted. These can stop us and reflect again on what fills our life. He was the victim of an assassination attempt in 1968 by Valerie Solanas. This changed him very much. In an article in "America: The Jesuit Review" (June 20, 2022) Angela Alaimo O'Donnell wrote an article "The Secret Catholic Life of Andy Warhol". She quotes a friend of Warhol's: "All his really important works were icons – figures to be venerated". Warhol was a gay man and felt an outsider. As a child he suffered many illnesses and had to spend much time at home. One of Warhol's last works was "The Last Supper Series". Among these were large-scale prints and silkscreens based on Da Vinci's work. Andy had his own via crucis.

In the eulogy in St. Patrick's Cathedral, John Richardson spoke to an audience of 3,000 people, many of them the glamorous celebrities Warhol sought out in life. Richardson said: "He attended Mass several times a week". He was responsible for conversions. He also helped pay for his nephew's journey to the priesthood. Richardson says: "Andy fooled the world into believing that his only obsession was money, fame and glamour and that he was cool to the point of callousness. In reality the callous observer was in fact a recording angel. And Andy's detachment – the distance he established between the world and himself – was above all a matter of innocence and art." He wore a cross around his neck and kept a rosary in his pocket. Andy would go to monthly confession. Once when he saw hungry people on the street he was deeply moved and gave of his time to work in a shelter serving meals to the homeless and the hungry. He also supported the soup kitchen financially. This soup kitchen was operated by the Church of the Heavenly Rest, an Episcopalian church on E. 90th street.

Warhol serving the homeless at the Church of the Heavenly Rest, New York. According to the rector, "Andy poured coffee, served food, and helped clean up. He was a true friend to these friendless. He loved these nameless New Yorkers and they loved him back."

Andy was a complex person with all his problems. He was also intensely shy which explains his reticence in talking about his work. This allows space for us to make up our own minds, not just say: "What did Andy mean?" His paintings of soup cans show us that our world is full of advertising and our image comes from this. His silkscreen works of violence show us what we have become used to in our lives. We take this violence for granted. Warhol makes us stop and think again.

In this work I try to present the alternative world of the Spirit. We do not meditate on the riches of the Holy Spirit in our lives. By reflecting on this way we allow the Spirit to enter our lives. St. Paul says: "The fruit of the Spirit is love, joy, peace, patience, kindness, generosity, faithfulness, gentleness, self-control" (Galatians 5:22f). This is the world we seek. Andy and his life show us that we are called, especially sinners. None of us are perfect. Yet we are the beloved of God. With sincere seeking we can enter this world of the Spirit. We have our struggles, questions and weaknesses. Yet this is the very place where we meet God.

Chapter One

Seeking

Jacob Bronowski was a famous scientific communicator. He made a set of programmes for the BBC called 'The Ascent of Man'. In one programme he says, if the early Biblical commentators were hi-tech they might say: "God made the neutron". He shows a nuclear reaction and the trace of the neutrons interacting with the uranium: "Here it is in the trace of the neutrons, the middle finger of God touching Adam in Michelangelo's painting, not with breath but with power."

This leads on to the next programme "Knowledge or Certainty", a meditation on World War II. He begins with a blind woman reading with her fingertip the face of an unidentified elderly man. She says: "It is not a happy face" – it is a face worn with anguish. She, at first, mistakes his wrinkles for scars.

The camera turns to Bronowski. He tells us that the principal aim of science has been to give us a God's eye view of the world. The great discovery of physics is to show us there is no such thing. Modern science now shows us there is no such thing. Science can only give us different ways of looking at reality. All of these provide information but the information depends on the questions asked. There is no One Genuine Truth in Physics from which we can divine other truths. Bronowski uses a trick he first employed at the 'Alice in Wonderland' Exhibit at the 1951 Festival of Britain showing what the man's face (the one we met earlier) looks like in different wavelengths of light. He uses infrared, a microscope and even with radar. At each scale different information is reached, but none captures the one perfect and total reality of the person.

The man is Stephan Borgrajewicz who was born in Poland like Bronowski. In 'The Ascent of Man', the BBC book following the series,[1] he shows paintings of Stephan by a Polish artist, Feliks Topolski.

---

[1] Jacob Bronowski, The Ascent of Man (BBC Books: 1975), p. 267.

We see a deeply lined face. Is this the real Stephen? No, but it gives information on Stephan that is not visible to the naked eye. The painter analyses the face, takes the features apart and enlarges the image.

He then looks at the world of Physics. He speaks of the astronomical observatory of Karl Friedrich Gauss at Göttingen, built about 1807. He speaks about how we look at the position of a star even with improved astronomical instruments. However, no matter how refined, there are always errors in our observations. We make an approximation of the star's position. Absolute knowledge eludes us. This is true of stars or atoms or just looking at somebody's face. We see this in the famed Gaussian curve – the spread of values. He looked at the star and the various readings and this gives him the spread of the curve.

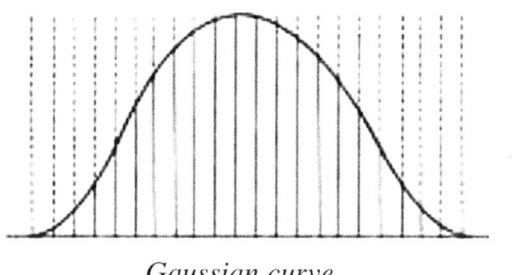
Gaussian curve.

There is an area of uncertainty. Error is bound up with our knowledge of the universe. Göttingen was the scene of great scientific exploration but then the Nazis came. The leading thinkers left and barbarism took over.

Scientists like Max Born, Erwin Schödinger and Werner Heisenberg did some of the last work at Göttingen. They looked at the world of sub-atomic particles and it turned out to be a world that is deeply mysterious and counter-intuitive. Max Born said when he came to England: "I am now convinced that theoretical physics is actual philosophy" (Ascent of Man, p. 276).

Leo Szilard was one who spent his university life in Germany but with the coming of the Nazis he had to leave. He did work on nuclear physics the the importance of the chain reaction. He wanted to keep his insights private. Einstein had shown the equivalence of mass and energy ($E = mc^2$). However, as war loomed he wrote a letter which Einstein signed and sent to President Roosevelt warning that nuclear energy is a reality.

In 1945 when the European war was won, he realised that the bomb was now about to be made and dropped on the Japanese. Szilard wanted the bomb to be tested openly before the Japanese so that the Japanese could see what they were up against. He hoped this would cause them to surrender. He tried to meet President Truman but he wasn't granted a hearing. After the war Bronowski worked in Japan assessing the damage the bomb had caused. Both he and Szilard were marked for life by the devastation caused. Szilard's failure was not seen by him as a failure for myself or scientists: "It is the tragedy of mankind" (Ascent, p. 284). Joan Baez's father was a famous scientist but he did not pursue career development by working for war programs. It is well known that if scientists are working on a project that will benefit humankind, funding can be difficult. If, however, they work on some way of arming and destroying others then funding turns up.

Bronowski speaks of the betrayal of the human spirit: the assertion of some dogma that closes the mind, and turns a nation, a civilisation, into a regiment of ghosts. It is said that science will dehumanise people and turn them into numbers. He said this is tragically false. He went to Auschwitz where people were turned into numbers. He looked at where the ashes of some four million people had been thrown. This was done by human beings who dehumanised others. It shows the death of the spirit and the agony of a people. He finishes the chapter by saying: "We have to touch people" (p. 286).

During the filming Bronowski wandered around the camp looking at the remains of those who died. This was actually his first time to visit the place where so many of his own relatives died. The closing sequence of 'The Ascent of Man' shows Bronowski at his most eloquent and profound. The atrocities of Nazism were not accomplished by science but by blind obedience, ignorance and a refusal to think independently. "Science is a tribute to what we can know although we are fallible."

Bronowski then stepped into a pool of water. The cameraman was caught off guard and pulled back to capture the unexpected gesture. "We have to cure ourselves of the itch for absolute knowledge and power." At this point the scene freezes and fades into one of the photos of the Jewish prisoners now on display at Auschwitz. The man is Stephan Borgrajewicz, the same man whose face had filled the scene at the episode's opening. The wrinkles that the blind woman mistook for scars are now explained, for he was a survivor of the camp. The episode ends in silence.

Looking for Spirituality:
Many of my generation sought to find a spiritual life. Some went east. I tried to find it in my own tradition. Since John XXII's time we have been directed to go to the sources of our spirituality and life. This is a journey that is ongoing. Ewart Cousins (+2009) was a professor at Fordham University. He was interested in interfaith dialogue. He was editor of a series on spirituality that had articles from scholars in the different faith traditions. The series focused on the inner dimensions of the person called by certain traditions "the spirit". This spiritual core is the deepest centre of the person. It is here that the person is open to the transcendent dimension; it is here that the person experiences ultimate reality. The series on spirituality explores the discovery of this core, the dynamics of its development and its journey to the ultimate goal. The series deals with prayer, spiritual direction, the maps of the spiritual journey.[2]

To follow what Cousins said here is in many ways counter-cultural. Charles de Foucauld is one such saint we will meet on our journey. In 1907 when he was in his hermitage at Tamanrasset he felt the pangs of loneliness and what looked like failure. He had dismissed for a time Paul Embarek with whom he had a troubled relationship. He could not say Mass unless he had a server and could not keep the Blessed Sacrament. On December 25, 1907, he reached the depths of despair. He

---

[2] see Ewert Cousins, A Spiritual Journey Into the Future (Lima, Ohio: 2010), p. 131. He wrote this originally in Philip Sheldrake, The New Westminster Dictionary of Christian Spirituality (Louisville, KY: 2005), p. 321-323.

had hoped someone would come to help him celebrate Christmas. He wrote to his cousin, Marie de Bondy: "Up to the last minute I hoped someone would come. But nothing came, no Christian traveler, no soldier, no permission to celebrate alone! For three months, more than three months I have received no letter. May the will of the Beloved be praised in everything."[3] He found himself in the dark night of the Spirit. His loneliness and his uselessness overpowered him.

Even in this loneliness his faith and love in Christ remained intact. He kept before himself the words of Saint John of the Cross: "It is precisely at the hour of the greatest prostration of the spirit that the Saviour discharges fully the debt of depraved man and effects our redemption."[4]

Some of his relatives judged him harshly. His cousin, General de Morlaincourt, said he was "a lunatic, a real lunatic". Even those who loved him unconditionally wanted him to come back to France. He was living in a miserable hermitage and was doomed to oblivion. He was completely alone. In 1908 when his health was failing he wrote in his diary: "Am sick, forced to interrupt my work. Jesus, Mary, Joseph, I give you my soul, my spirit and my life" (Carnets de Tamanrasset, p. 87).

In his illness he received a great kindness. A Targui, one of the people he had been kind to, had seen he was unwell. The man gave a cup of goat's milk, whispering with affection and respect: "Sidi Marabout". Then he added fervently: "Khaouia Carlo". Charles had always shared the little he had. Now those he had shared with saw he was ill and they made great sacrifices to get the goat's milk to help Charles build up his strength.

In the autumn Bishop Guérin had written to the Pope to try and get permission for Charles to say Mass. Also Father Burtin, procurator general of the White Fathers, met with the Pope, told him of Charles living among the Tuareg and requested permission. This was granted. Charles recovered and his spirit was restored.

---

[3] Jean-Jacques Antier, Charles de Foucauld (Paris: 1997), p. 351.
[4] Quoted by M. Castillon du Perron, Charles de Foucauld (Grasset: 1982), p. 397.

We will meet Charles again later. His journey in the Spirit and his exploration of new ways of living with people of other faiths is something those seeking spirituality, life in the Spirit, can hold onto. There are many pitfalls and disappointments on the way but God works through even these. Many give up the search because of disappointment. People like Charles teach us as much as we seek God he seeks us even more. We have to let him work in his own time. Eventually Charles's life touched others and led them to find God. He inspired others in their journey in the Spirit.

Beginning the Journey of the Spirit:
Teresa of Avila wrote "The Interior Castle" to guide us in prayer. The idea of a castle came to her mind in the task of writing about prayer. She asks us to consider our soul to be like a castle made entirely of diamonds – very clear crystal in which there are many rooms. She marvels at the beauty and value of our souls created in the image and likeness of God.

> "…we realise that the soul of the just person is nothing else but a paradise where the Lord says he finds His delight."
> (Interior Castle, 1:1)

She says later:

> "His Majesty in saying that the soul is made in His own image makes it almost impossible for us to understand the sublime dignity and beauty of the soul."
> (Interior Castle, 1:1)

She laments that we don't understand ourselves or know who we are. We are more concerned with "the outer wall of the castle; that is with these bodies of ours" (Interior Castle, 1:2). Compare this with the way Stephan Borgrajewicz and so many others were viewed. Teresa pointed out our infinite dignity. The Nazis were killers of the spirit. Saints like Teresa teach us differently. Even in spirituality we hear so many people deprecate us, reminding us of our sinfulness. Teresa doesn't do this but points out we have an inner dignity and are called to a deep communion with God to allow him restore our dignity and lead us to eternal life. She points out that there are many rooms in our souls. Prayer is the means by which we enter the castle of our souls and leads us to peace with God. Prayer is a loving dialogue with one we know who loves us. In the beginning prayer can be mental or vocal. Teresa shows us a different way than we saw in the way people were treated in Bronowski's chapter in "The Ascent of Man". Indeed it is very different from the way our society looks at different people.

In this castle, as we said, there are many dwelling 'places' and in the centre is the place where sweet exchanges take place between God and the soul. We begin with prayer to enter this place. Prayer involves attention to God, the one who loves and accepts us. The Catechism of the Catholic Church says, in the spirit of Teresa:

> "Being in the image of God the human individual possesses the dignity of a person, who is not just something, but someone. He is capable of self-knowledge, of self-possession and of freely giving himself and entering into communion with other persons. And he is called by grace to a covenant with his Creator, to offer him a response of faith and love that no other creature can give in his stead."
> (Catechism, 357).

In being made in the image and likeness of God we have a capacity for God, Teresa says, that transcends the human person. Not only are we called to communion with God, but we are formed in such a way that God lives in us as his own dwelling place, more so than he does in the whole cosmos. Teresa's insights are supported by the words of sacred scripture. We see: "In my Father's house there are many dwelling places" (Jn 14:2), "I found my delight in the human race" (Proverbs 8:31) and "Let us make humankind in our image, after our likeness" (Genesis 1:26). These texts became part of Teresa's life and her convictions.

Blaise Pascal (+1662) spoke of the "misère et grandeur de l'homme" (the misery and grandeur of men). He speaks of the misery of the human predicament. We fall short of who we are called to be. Yet we have a unique grandeur in being loved by God and we are called to a higher dignity. In embracing the spiritual world we enter that healing process. Pascal pointed out that much of our trouble begins because we cannot spend time alone in silence (Pensées, 1 - Brunschvicg edition). Andrea Bocelli wrote his autobiography "The Music of Silence".[5] Bocelli speaks of music as a fundamental need of the human person, like love. It is his destiny to sing. He tells the story of how, when he went to the Maestro, his teacher, to learn his art, he was told to be silent and allow the music come from the very depths of his being. Then he could sing. By analogy we can see what this means for our spiritual life. In silence we can let the Spirit speak to our spirit and allow the image of God shine forth. In silence Andrea got in touch with who he truly was and his gift. (The Music of Silence, p. 208ff).

St. Teresa wrote a poem about how we come to know ourselves and what we are called to in God's love.

> **Yours I am, born yours to be,**
> **what's your will to make of me?**
>
> Sovereign Majesty, decreeing
> wisdom timeless, ever whole;
> kindness pleasing to my soul;
> God, most high, all good, one being,
> this vile creature you are seeing,
> who sings to you lovingly:
> *what's your will to make of me?*
>
> Yours, for me you did create,
> Yours, since me you did succor,
> Yours, since me you did endure,
> Yours, you called me to my fate,
> Yours, for me you did long wait,
> Yours, I chose not lost to be.
> *What's your will to make of me?*

---

[5] Andrea Bocelli, The Music of Silence (New Jersey: 2011).

What, then, is your will, good Lord,
that this servant vile should do?
What work can you give unto
this poor slave in sin abhorred?
Look at me, sweet Love adored,
sweet Love, here for you to see,
What's your will to make of me?

See my heart here for inspection,
I place it within your hand,
with my body, life, soul and
my deep feelings and affection,
sweetest Bridegroom and redemption,
myself offering yours to be,
What's your will to make of me?

Give me death, or let me live,
give health or infirmity,
shame or honor give to me,
war or peace to me now give,
weakness, strength superlative,
to all these I will agree,
What's your will to make of me?

Give me wealth or poverty,
give relief or troubled spell,
give me sorrow or give glee,
give me heaven or give me hell,
sweet life or sun without veil,
I surrender totally.
What's your will to make of me?

If you wish to, give me prayer,
if not, give me dryness too,
if abundant worship fair,
if not barrenness will do,
Sovereign Majesty, in you
I find all my peace to be.
What's your will to make of me?

Give me wisdom's deep insight,
or for love, just ignorance,
give me years of abundance,
or of hunger, famine's blight,
give me dark or clear daylight,
move me here or there freely.
What's your will to make of me?

If you wish that I should rest,
I, for love, want to rest to savor;
if your will is that I labor,
death from work is my request.
Say where, how, when, manifest;
say, sweet Love, now say clearly.
What's your will to make of me?

Give me Tabor or Calvary,
desert or land fruitfully fine,
be as Job in misery,
of John, on your breast recline;
let me be a fruitful vine
or bare, as your will may be.
What's your will to make of me?

Be I Joseph placed in chains,
Egypt's governor of renown,
or as David suffering pains,
or now David bearing crown,
be I Jonah nearly drowned,
or from waters now set free,
what's your will to make of me?

Being silent, moved to speak,
bearing fruit or barren woe,
my wound to me law does show,
Gospel mild does joy bespeak;
mournful or enjoyment's peak,
in me now lives You only,
what's your will to make of me?

*Yours I am, born yours to be,
what's your will to make of me?*

~ A poem by Saint Teresa of Ávila

The New Spirit:
George Bernanos, the French writer, often spoke of sincerity. He said: "Saint Francis and Saint Dominic had first to offer themselves in sacrifice to prove that this new way was possible. For such is the lot God reserves for his saints" (Dominique, p. 23). These saints attracted people by their genuineness. Those who came to them found healing, acceptance and strength. They showed a new way is possible.

> "Whoever pretends to reform the Church with ... the same means used to reform temporal society: not only will he fail in his undertaking, but he will infallibly end by finding himself outside the Church. I say that he finds himself outside the Church before anyone has gone to the trouble of excluding him from her. I say that it is he himself who excludes himself from her by a kind of tragic fatalism... The only way of reforming the Church is to suffer for her. The only way of reforming the visible Church is to suffer for the invisible Church. The only way of reforming the vices of the Church is to lavish on her the example of one's own most heroic virtues.
>
> It's quite possible that Saint Francis of Assisi was not any less thrown into revolt than Luther by the debauchery and simony of prelates. We can even be sure that his suffering on this account was fiercer, because his nature was very different from that of the monk of Wittenberg. But Francis did not challenge iniquity; he was not tempted to confront it; instead, he threw himself into poverty, immersing himself in it as deeply as possible along with his followers. He found in poverty the very source and wellspring of all absolution and all purity. Instead of attempting to snatch from the Church all her ill-gotten goods, he overwhelmed

> her with invisible treasures, and under the hand of this beggar the heaps of gold and lust began blossoming like an April hedge. Ah, yes: I'm well aware that in these matters comparisons aren't worth much, especially when seasoned with a little humour. Would you still allow me to say, however, in order to be better understood by some readers, that what the Church needs is not critics but artists?.., When poetry is in full crisis, the important thing is not to point the finger at bad poets but oneself to write beautiful poems, thus unstopping the sacred springs."
>
> (Esprit, October 1951, p. 989f)

When poetry is in full crisis, the important thing is to write something beautiful. What a way to describe what Francis did. In living authentically he drew others to himself and this led to the healing of the Church. Needless to say there were other visionaries but his influence continues down through the centuries. He shows us life in the Spirit is possible and can still inspire. Bernanos pointed out that the saints lived and suffered like the rest of us. But they were called by God and lived with Him in the world we live in. They saw the suffering of the world but this did not lead them to rebellion but to care for those in agony and distress.

> "But, compared to the small number of those who experience a sincere revolt, how many others are there who, in their revolt against suffering, are only looking for a more or less sly justification for their own indifference and selfishness in the face of those who suffer? If this were not so, then by what miracle does it happen that precisely those who accept the most humbly, and without understanding it, the permanent scandal of suffering and misery are almost always the very same ones who devote themselves the most tenderly to the care of the suffering and miserable, for instance, Saint Francis of Assisi and Saint Vincent de Paul."[6]
>
> (Liberté, Pourquoi Faire? p. 278-280)

---

[6] The quotes from Bernanos are found in Hans Urs Von Balthasar, Bernanos: An Ecclesial Existence (San Francisco: 1999).

What led others to rebellion led people like the saints to reach out and bind up the wounds of the broken. They show another way is possible.

Saint Francis (+1226) tells us of his experience. In the very first lines of his 'Testament', written shortly before his death, we read:

> "In this way did the Lord give me, Brother Francis, the grace to begin doing penance: when I was in sin, it seemed too bitter for me to see lepers. And the Lord Himself led me among them and I showed mercy to them. And when I left them, what had seemed bitter to me was changed into sweetness of soul and body. And afterwards I delayed a little and left the world."

The foundation of his conversion was his experience of the Spirit leading him among the lepers. It was the door to a deeper compassion. His coming to embrace the leper was, for him, the result of the Spirit's moving. St. Francis encouraged those who followed him to discover the same experience. He said: "And they must rejoice when they live among people who are considered of little worth and who are looked down upon, among the poor and the powerless, the sick and the lepers, and the beggars by the wayside." (Earlier Rule, ch. 9). In this way we should share "to follow the humility and poverty of Our Lord Jesus Christ".

As he embraced the leper, Francis was led to Christ. He was inspired by the Holy Spirit. He felt the presence of the Lord leading him to them. He saw God living in the poor and downcast. This leading by the Holy Spirit was important to Francis. In chapter 10 of the Late Rule he wrote that his brothers "must desire above all things to have the spirit of the Lord and his holy manner of working."

The Holy Spirit, which Francis desired, led him to identify with the mortified and crucified flesh of the Christ and this defended him from the desire of power, control or domination of another. His eyes were focussed on "the Good Shepherd who suffered the passion of the cross to save his sheep" (Admonition, 4). Francis identified his life and the life of the brothers as "the life of the gospel of Jesus Christ". The Spirit that led him among the lepers also revealed that he should live with his brothers "the life of the Gospel of Jesus Christ" (Testament). He revered the Word of God in the Sacred Scripture. He said these were "Spirit and Life". Sacred Scripture was the voice of the Son of God and his life was to hold fast to the holy words.

The Jesus of the Gospels, who handed himself over to accepting death (Philippians 2:8) and spoke his words of love, was also present in Francis's eyes in the Eucharist, in the sacrament of his body and blood. Humility allows the Spirit of the Lord, dwelling within, to receive "the most holy body and blood of the Lord." Only with the eyes of the Spirit can one see him. He now humbles himself under the form of bread and wine and is now present always to us. In the first Admonition of Saint Francis we see it is by the Spirit that we hear his voice in the Gospel and it is by the same Spirit that we come to perceive his presence in the Eucharist.

> "Why will you not know the truth and "believe in the Son of God?" Behold daily He humbles Himself as when from His "royal throne" He came into the womb of the Virgin; daily He Himself comes to us with like humility; daily He descends from the bosom of His Father upon the altar in the hands of the priest. And as He appeared in true flesh to the Holy Apostles, so now He shows Himself to us in the sacred Bread; and as they by means of their fleshly eyes saw only His flesh, yet contemplating Him with their spiritual eyes, believed Him to be God, so we, seeing bread and wine with bodily eyes, see and firmly believe it to be His most holy Body and true and living Blood. And in this way our Lord is ever with His faithful, as He Himself says: "Behold I am with you all days, even to the consummation of the world.""

The Spirit of the Lord which led him among the lepers led him to Mont La Verna two years before his death. He received the wounds of Christ crucified in his body. St. Bonaventure, a future follower of Saint Francis, wrote of the wounds Francis received (called the stigmata): He was "totally transformed into the likeness of Christ crucified, not by the martyrdom of his flesh, but by the fire of his love consuming his soul" (13:12).

Soon after his experience of God on Mont La Verna, Francis composed 'The Canticle of Creation'. This poetic hymn was written when he was nearly blind and in great pain. He praises life in the Most High and he is at peace with God. He is at peace with all the elements of the Cosmos because he sees them with the eyes of the Spirit. All the elements of the world with one voice praise God the Most High. He is in love with all that there is and his compassion embraces all. He died in 1226. He loved to let God's Spirit move him. To many they felt drawn by him and longed to share his spirit. Many saints followed him – in his own time there were people like Clare of Assisi, Angela of Foligno, Anthony of Padua and Bonaventure. It is true that over the years many who followed Francis fell very short of his vision. Yet Francis's life and vision continues to call and challenge. There are still many who share in his spirit. Charles de Foucauld (+1916) brought to life much of the vision of Saint Francis. Both show that there is another way of life possible than the vision of the modern world. Auschwitz represented a death of the Spirit. There is still the vision of Francis led by the Holy Spirit which shows us there is another vision!

Kierkegaard (+1855), in his study of scripture and in his writing, spoke of being contemporaneous with the world of scripture. That is, we study scripture and see how to make what it teaches real in our modern life. Ewert Cousins (+2009) spoke of the "Mysticism of the Historical Event".[7] In this type of consciousness one recalls a significant event in the past, enters into the drama and draws from it spiritual energy, moving beyond the event to union with God. For Christians the events of Jesus's life, the birth at Bethlehem and his death and resurrection, are central. This was always present in Christianity. In Francis it gets a new impetus. It developed into a form of meditative prayer which continued down through the centuries. One imagines the physical setting of the

---

[7] Ewert Cousins, A Spiritual Journey Into the Future (Lima, Ohio: 2010), p. 45-48. This was originally printed in Mysticism and Religious Traditions, Steven Katz (Oxford: 1983), p. 166-169.

event – the place, the persons, the circumstances, for example the birth of Jesus at Bethlehem, with Mary and Joseph, an ox and an ass. In Greccio in 1223, Francis helped the people recall Jesus's birth. They celebrated by acting out the events of Bethlehem. Francis had a good friend, Giovanni Vellita, who was in charge of Greccio and had fallen under Francis's spell. Francis said he wanted to set "before our eyes the hardships of his infant needs, how he lay in the manger..." People prepared torches and candles to light up the night. The manger was prepared in a cave with a real ox and ass brought in. On Christmas Eve the people came in procession, carrying their torches and candles. The woods rang with their song. They were rediscovering the joy of childhood. This was the beginning of the tradition of the crib at Christmas season. This form of meditation ground its way into Saint Ignatius of Loyola's (+1556) "Spiritual Exercises".

This mysticism of the Historical Event makes the event present to us and we to the event. In and through our immersion in the event we begin to discover its meaning as it reveals God's plan of salvation history and through this history meet God himself. This consciousness is different from everyday consciousness. We transcend the present moment and we find the inner meaning of the past in the present. This is why Cousins calls it "mysticism".

Francis was attracted to Christ crucified and the marks of Jesus crucified were found on his body. Saint Bonaventure (+1274) was a successor of Saint Francis. The order was wracked with divisions and Bonaventure tried to find a middle way to heal the divisions. He went to Mont La Verna to find peace. Bonaventure wrote his masterpiece "The Journey of the Mind to God" (Itinerarium Mentis ad Deum) there. He mentions this time in La Verna and how he found peace. "While I was there reflecting on various ways by which the soul ascends into God, there came to mind among other things, the miracle which had occurred to Blessed Francis in this very place: the vision of a winged Seraph in the form of the Crucified. While reflecting on this, I saw at once this vision represented our Father's rapture in contemplation and the road by which this rapture is reached." The completion of the journey in contemplative rapture is intimacy with Christ crucified. This is the fulfillment of

Francis's journey. Bonaventure says: "With Christ crucified let us pass out of this world to the Father so that when it is shown to us, we say with Philip: It is enough for us." The following of Christ is fulfilled in contemplation. It is the entrance of the person of Christ to his father.

This devotion to Christ's birth and death were part of the "Mysticism of the Historical Event". This devotion to the humanity of Christ found expression in the life of the people, in literature and art. Under the influence of Saint Francis artists began to depict the human Jesus suffering. Francis was a charismatic figure who showed us Jesus's humanity. The building of Franciscan churches continued. Franciscans told the people who often couldn't read or write of the events of Christ's life or the life of a saint. Andrew Graham-Dixon in his TV series and the book following the TV series, Renaissance, sees in this the seeds of what we came to call the Renaissance.[8] Karl Barth (+1968) kept a painting of the crucifixion by Matthias Grünewald. This helped always to see the real suffering of the human Jesus.

Bonaventure says of this:

> There is no other path but through the burning love of the Crucified, a love which so transformed Paul into Christ when he "was carried up to the third heaven" (2 Cor 12:2) that he could say: "With Christ I am nailed to the cross. I live, now not I, but Christ lives in me" (Gal 2:20). This love also so absorbed the soul of Francis that his spirit shone through his flesh when for two years before his death he carried in his body the sacred stigmata of the passion. The six wings of the Seraph, therefore, symbolize the six steps of illumination that begin from creatures and lead up to God, whom no one rightly enters except through the Crucified. For "he who enters not through the door, but climbs up another way is a their and a robber." But "if anyone enter" through this door, "he will go in and out and will find pastures" (John 10:1, 9). Therefore John says in the Apocalypse: "Blessed are they who wash their robes in

---

[8] Andrew Graham-Dixon (BBC, London: 1999), p. 18-35.

the blood of the Lamb that they may have a right to the tree of life and may enter the city through the gates" (Apoc 22:14). It is as if John were saying that no one can enter the heavenly Jerusalem by contemplation unless he enter through the blood of the Lamb as through a door.

(Journey, prol. 3)

In the seventh chapter of the Journey (Itinerarium) Bonaventure deals with the passage of the soul into God in ecstasy. He bids the reader to turn his gaze on the humanity of Christ, symbolised by the Mercy Seat in the Holy of Holies in the Temple: "Whoever turns his face fully to the Mercy Seat and with faith, hope and love, devotion, admiration, exultation, appreciation, praise and joy beholds him hanging upon the Cross, such a one makes the Pasch, the Passover with Christ." When we die to ourselves with Christ and come to union with him we hear the words said to the thief on the cross: "Today you shall be with me in Paradise" (Luke 23:43), (Journey, 7:2). This is the journey the Spirit leads us on.

Chapter 2

All is Grace
'Tout est Grâce'

This was something that Thérèse of Lisieux (+1897) said (MsA, 38v - 39r). She had faith and confidence that God worked through all things that happened in her life. George Bernanos (+1948), at the conclusion of his book 'The Diary of a Country Priest' (Journal d'un curé de Campagne) (1936), said at the end: 'All is Grace' (Tout est grâce). We have become unaccustomed to speaking about grace and the Holy Spirit. He is the source of all grace. St. Thérèse helps us understand the message of St. James: "Every good and perfect gift is from above, coming down from the Father of the heavenly lights, who does not change like shifting shadows" (James 1:17).

In Exodus 28:1-3 Moses sets Aaron aside as the one who is to be priest for the people – he and his sons. In Ex 28:3 the translation goes as follows: "And you shall speak to all the wise of heart, whom I have filled with the Spirit of Wisdom, and they will make Aaron's vestments (Ex 28:3).[1] Israel's prophets and priests are inspired. They are skilled because they are already filled with a Spirit of Wisdom. The Hebrew word (ml') means being filled with the Spirit from the inside out. In Exodus 31:1-6 and Exodus 36 – 39 Bezalel was the chief artisan of the Tabernacle. The name 'Bezalel' means "in the shadow [protection] of God". Oholiab was appointed to help him (Ex 31:6). His craft was a gift of God and he used his craft to beautify the place of worship. God is present in all our gifts, our blessings and our trials. We read in Ex 35:

> Then Moses said to the Israelites: See, the Lord has called by name Bezalel son of Uri son of Hur, of the tribe of Judah; he has filled him with divine Spirit, with skill, intelligence, and knowledge in every kind of craft, to devise

[1] see Jack Levison, 40 Days with the Holy Spirit (Paraclete Press: 2023).

artistic designs, to work in gold, silver, and bronze, in cutting stones for setting, and in carving wood, in every kind of craft. And he has inspired him to teach, both him and Oholiab sone of Ahisamach, of the tribe of Dan. He has filled them with skill to do every kind of work done by an artisan or by a designer or by an embroiderer in blue and purple, and crimson yarns, and in fine linen, or by a weaver – by any sort of artisan or skilled designer.

(Exodus 35:30-35)

We read in the Book of Job that "there is a spirit in man: and the inspiration of the Almighty gives them understanding" (Job 32:8).

Leontyne Price (born 1927) is an American spinto soprano who was the first African American soprano to receive international acclaim. From 1961 she began a long association with the Metropolitan Opera. She has appeared in many of the leading opera houses of the world including La Scala in Milan. She is renowned for her performance in the lead role of Verdi's 'Aida'. She believes that when she sings she is in communion with the Spirit of God. He is with her. The following is what she said about her singing:[2]

> Singing is a very personal art form. An instrumentalist has to deal with, and touch, another object – a violin, a piano, etc. However, singers are the object of the art, and singing is the most personal way to express art. It is you, and you are it. The breath that is involved with singing is a technical thing. It is part of the training that helps to produce the voice in the best form possible. But breath, in terms of the Spirit of God, is really about the sense I get of being in the hands of God when I sing. I really do feel that I am in touch with something much higher than myself, and much higher than the performance that I am giving. I am in the hands of God, who guides me far beyond any technical expertise that I may have.

---

[2] see Joanna Laufer and Kenneth S. Lewis, Inspired: The Breath of God (New York: 1998). These are conversations they had with gifted people about their faith and inspiration. This interview is found on p. 17f.

I never go out on the stage without praying. I have to have that moment before I go on stage, because I will not go out without letting God know that I need His strength. One night I was supposed to perform, and I was very ill. This happened in Dallas. It was the opening of the wonderful new hall there, in 1989. My recital was supposed to be the first one held there. As always, I took time to pray before, and somehow I was able to get to the stage. I leaned on the piano because I was very weak and ill, and I prayed silently after each note, as if saying to God, "It's really not up to me alone. It's up to you and me." I will always remember that night because I probably did the best singing I have ever done. With every note, I felt God's presence. After the performance, I was taken to hospital and diagnosed with diverticulitis.

I think that all artists are vessels, and that we are guided in the way that we express our art. I feel so grateful to God that He gave me the gift of being able to sing. I cannot believe that any artist does not acknowledge that his or her art was a gift from God. It has been said of the composer Giuseppe Verdi that he was an agnostic. I do not believe that you can compose the Verdi *Requiem* and be an agnostic. *Libera me, Domine* ("Deliver me, O Lord"). How can you include that without knowing to whom you are speaking? Who are you asking to free you? Who are you asking for salvation? There is only one God, and if you put yourself in the hands of God you *will* be free. Whenever I sang the *Requiem*, my own experiences and my total belief in the omnipotent merged so completely. Conductors have told me that it seemed as if I were having an out-of-body experience when I sang it – that I was someplace else, though, of course, always in the music, but outside of just the notes. In every performance that I have ever done of Verdi's *Requiem*, it felt as if God wrote every note.

In God we "live and move and have our being" (Acts 17:28). Everything is upheld by God's creative hand. The Holy Spirit breathes life into our gifts and gives them life. Here Paul quotes ancient Greek poetic literature.

Ang Lee is a Taiwanese filmmaker. He was educated in Taiwan and later in the United States. As a filmmaker Lee's work is known for its emotional charge and exploration of repressed, hidden emotions. His breakthrough in Hollywood was the acclaimed costume drama 'Sense and Sensibility' (1995). He went on to receive the Academy Award for best director twice – for 'Brokeback Mountain' (2005) and for 'The Life of Pi' (2012). While preparing to work he meditates in silence with those he works with to let the creative energies flow. He describes how he came to do this in the book 'Inspired: The Breath of God'.

> I believe that all we create is sent from somewhere. It is as if our ideas already exist, and pass through us in order to be seen. What is up in the air comes down and comes through you. If a movie works, it has a life of its own. The director's job is to find the life of the movie, and when it comes alive with the audiences, it is out of the director's hands. Once the movie goes to the theatre, I hardly feel anything, even watching it. It has used me, and then it is gone.
>
> All my life, when things have happened that have worked out successfully, it has been because of what has come to me, not from what I have willed. However, in my thirties, I was not having success. I didn't get work for six years. This was very tough to go through as a filmmaker, a struggling artist. Many scripts and projects did not work out for me. I walked around a lot every day. It was a very difficult time. At night it was very hard to fall asleep. I would look at the stars, and feel how big the universe is, and how small we are. Universal laws, natural laws, do exist, and are beyond human understanding. Seeing how meaningless existence can be sort of lightened up my burden, and helped me pass through these years.
>
> During this time, I began to read books about Buddhism, which were very enlightening. I started meditating and doing tai chi, which helped me calm down. I feel totally

religious, but not in a formal way. I think balance is the key, not going to any extreme. This is very Chinese. As a human being, I would like to be humble, to try to keep a balance, and to observe what is going on beyond this life. I believe that the best ideas and inspiration come from something beyond us, from something that is above us, rotating. When I try to force my ideas to fit an agenda, it never works.

(Inspired: The Breath of God, p. 108)

Inspiration, for Lee, comes from he does not know where. When he tries to force his ideas he sees that if he tries to force his ideas then he knows things aren't working. He has to follow his inspiration.

Flannery O'Connor (+1964) was an American novelist, short story writer and essayist. She was from Savannah, Georgia, US. She wrote of the Holy Spirit working through our gifts. She said:

> Even if one were filled with the Holy Ghost, the Holy Ghost would work through the given talent. You see this in Biblical inspiration, so why think that it would be different in a lesser kind of inspiration? If the Holy Ghost dictated a novel, I doubt very much that all would be flow. I doubt that the writer would be relieved of his capacity for taking pains (which is all that technique is in the end); I doubt that he would lose the habit of art. I think it would only be perfected. The greater the love, the greater the pains he would take.[3]

Madeleine L'Engle (+2007) was another American writer of fiction, poetry and young adult fiction. She spoke of prayer in her work. She did not see prayer as a monologue. St. Teresa spoke of prayer as a dialogue, a conversation with one who loves us. The Holy Spirit is at work. L'Engle said:

> To work on a book is for me very much the same thing as to pray. Both involve discipline. If the artist works only

---

[3] Sally Fitzgerald (ed.), The Habit of Being: Letters of Flannery O'Connor (New York: 1979), p. 387.

when he feels like it, he's not apt to build up much of a body of work. Inspiration far more often comes during the work than before it, because the largest part of the job of an artist is to listen to the work, and to go where it tells him to go. Ultimately, when you are writing, you stop thinking and write what you hear. To pray is to listen also, to move through my own chattering to God, to that place where I can be silent and listen to what God may have to say.[4]

Antonin Dvorák (+1904) saw his work as being inspired by God. He was a Czech composer. He spoke of his talents as "God's voice". He went on: "I simply do what God tells me to do".[5] He said he studied music with the birds, flowers, trees, God and himself. His faith also supported him in difficult times. His first three children died in infancy and his faith kept him going in the face of this tragedy. He poured out his grief in his composition 'Stabat Mater'. This refers to Mary grieving at the foot of the Cross.

The Holy Spirit:
"The wind blows where it wishes, and you hear its sound, but you do not know where it comes from or where it goes. So it is with everyone who is born of the Spirit."
(John 3:8)

The Greek word for wind is *pneuma*. It is the same word used for Spirit. John plays on the double sense of *pneuma* here. *Pneuma* translates the Hebrew word '*ruach*'.[6] The word in Hebrew means wind, breath or spirit. It originally meant wind with its dynamic energy. You see its

---

[4] Madeleine L'Engle, Walking on Water: Reflections on Faith and Art (Wheaton, Illinois: 1980), p. 149.

[5] Patrick Kavanaugh, The Spiritual Lives of Great Composers (Nashville: 1992), p. 77.

[6] For a study of 'ruach' see Francis Brown, with S. R. Driver and C. A. Briggs (ads.), The New Hebrew and English Lexicon (Lafayette, IN.: Associated Publishers, 1980), pp. 924-26; G. J. Botterweck and H. Ringgren (eds.), Theological Dictionary of the Old Testament (TDOT) (Grand Rapids: Eerdmans, 1980), vol. 2, p. 836; W. Van Gemeren (ed.), New International Dictionary of Old Testament Theology and Exegesis 9NIDOTTE), 5 vols. (Carlisle: Paternoster, 1997), vol. 3, p. 1073.

effects. Over time this 'ruach' came to mean Spirit. It is like the breath that gives birth to words. This Spirit can rest on a person (Isaiah 11).

We see in Genesis the idea of the breath of life:

> "The Lord God formed the human from the dust of the ground and breathed into his nostrils the breath of life, and the human begin became a living creature."
>
> (Gen 2:7)

As human beings we are creatures who have the breath of life. We are all uniquely created in God's own image and called to a special intimacy with God. It is the work of the Spirit that generates all that makes life special. Job reflects on the relationship with God's spirit who gives life and human capacity.

> "As long as I have life within me,
> the breath of God in my nostrils,
> my lips will not speak wickedness."
>
> (Job 27:3-4)

> "But it is the spirit in a man,
> the breath of the Almighty, that gives him understanding."
>
> (Job 32:8)

> "The Spirit of God has made me;
> the breath of the Almighty gives me life."
>
> (Job 33:4)

Yet in Genesis 3 we see how human beings fell from grace and death entered the world.

This giving of life takes on another meaning in the prophet Ezekiel. Ezekiel has a vision of the dry bones but the breath of God, the Spirit, comes upon them and brings them to life. This vision refers to the restoration of Israel and Judah to their homeland. The passage reads:

The hand of the LORD was on me, and he brought me out by the Spirit of the LORD and set me in the middle of a valley; it was full of bones. He led me back and forth among them, and I saw a great many bones on the floor of the valley, bones that were very dry. He asked me, "Son of man, can these bones live?"

I said, "Sovereign LORD, you alone know."

Then he said to me, "Prophesy to these bones and say to them, 'Dry bones, hear the word of the LORD!
This is what the Sovereign LORD says to these bones:
I will make breath enter you, and you will come to life.
I will attach tendons to you and make flesh come upon you and cover you with skin; I will put breath in you, and you will come to life. Then you will know that I am the LORD.'"

So I prophesied as I was commanded. And as I was prophesying, there was a noise, a rattling sound, and the bones came together, bone to bone. I looked, and tendons and flesh appeared on them and skin covered them, but there was no breath in them.

Then he said to me, "Prophesy to the breath; prophesy, son of man, and say to it, 'This is what the Sovereign LORD says: Come, breath, from the four winds and breathe into these slain, that they may live.'"

So I prophesied as he commanded me, and breath entered them; they came to life and stood up on their feet—a vast army.

Then he said to me: "Son of man, these bones are the people of Israel. They say, 'Our bones are dried up and our hope is gone; we are cut off.' Therefore prophesy and say to them: 'This is what the Sovereign LORD says: My people, I am going to open your graves and bring you up from them; I will bring you back to the land of Israel. Then you, my people, will know that I am the LORD, when I open your graves and bring you up from them. I will put my Spirit in you and you will live, and I will settle you in your own land. Then you will know that I the LORD have spoken, and I have done it, declares the LORD.'"

(Ezekiel 37:1-14)

In this vision Ezekiel announces the restoration of Judah and Israel who are now in exile. The Spirit brings hope and a new beginning is possible. This is the promise of hope in the future in spite of all that seems to be against hope.

The Spirit gives life to our spirit too. He helps us turn to God and walk in his ways. Psalm 51 is an example of this. It is attributed to David when he repents of his adultery. The first verses show his repentance:

> For the director of music. A psalm of David. when the prophet Nathan came to him after David had committed adultery with Bathsheba.
>
> Have mercy on me, O God,
> according to your unfailing love;
> according to your great compassion
> blot out my transgressions.
> Wash away all my iniquity
> and cleanse me from my sin.
> For I know my transgressions,
> and my sin is always before me.
> Against you, you only, have I sinned
> and done what is evil in your sight;
> so you are right in your verdict
> and justified when you judge.
> Surely I was sinful at birth,
> sinful from the time my mother conceived me.
> Yet you desired faithfulness even in the womb;
> you taught me wisdom in that secret place.
> (Ps 51:1-6)

He confronts his own failures and weaknesses. He places all his sin in the hands of God. In doing so he experiences forgiveness and healing. He is accepted. The psalm continues:

> Cleanse me with hyssop, and I will be clean;
> wash me, and I will be whiter than snow.

> Let me hear joy and gladness;
> > let the bones you have crushed rejoice.
> Hide your face from my sins
> > and blot out all my iniquity.
> Create in me a pure heart, O God,
> > and renew a steadfast spirit within me.
> Do not cast me from your presence
> > or take your Holy Spirit from me.
> Restore to me the joy of your salvation
> > and grant me a willing spirit, to sustain me.
>
> (Ps 51:7-12)

He prays not to let God's Spirit depart from him. It is an act of faith in God's mercy. That is why he can give all to God. This opens up for him a new way of being. He prays to come to know the joy of God's salvation.

> Then I will teach transgressors your ways,
> > so that sinners will turn back to you.
> Deliver me from the guilt of bloodshed, O God,
> > you who are God my Savior,
> > and my tongue will sing of your righteousness.
> Open my lips, Lord,
> > and my mouth will declare your praise.
> You do not delight in sacrifice, or I would bring it;
> > you do not take pleasure in burnt offerings.
> My sacrifice, O God, is a broken spirit;
> > a broken and contrite heart
> > you, God, will not despise.
>
> (Ps 51:13-17)

He offers God his humble and contrite spirit. He knows this will be accepted. This allows him to praise God, walk in his ways and call others to this place of peace.

At the very beginning of the Bible in the Book of Genesis we read:

> In the beginning God created the heavens and the earth. Now the earth was formless and empty, darkness was over the surface of the deep, and the Spirit of God was hovering over the waters.
>
> And God said, "Let there be light," and there was light. God saw that the light was good, and he separated the light from the darkness. God called the light "day," and the darkness he called "night." And there was evening, and there was morning—the first day.
>
> (Gen 1:1-5)

The Spirit of God (ruach elohim in Hebrew here) hovers over the waters – the chaos of the formless void. In modern physics the Big Bang Theory refers to the first moments of the formation of the universe. It too is a hot dense chaos from which order springs. We see God's power in creation. Job links together God's power, wisdom, breath, hand and "whisper" in the great work of creation. All these work together:

> By his power he churned up the sea;
>   by his wisdom he cut Rahab to pieces.
> By his breath the skies became fair;
>   his hand pierced the gliding serpent.
> And these are but the outer fringe of his works;
>   how faint the whisper we hear of him!
>   Who then can understand the thunder of his power?"
>
> (Job 26:12-14)

In the passage from Genesis we see the link between spirit and word. The word expresses the spirit and creation comes to be: "Let there be Light" (Gen 1:3).

Ps 33 celebrates the create of God. We read:

> For the word of the Lord is right and true;
>   he is faithful in all he does.
> The Lord loves righteousness and justice;
>   the earth is full of his unfailing love.

> By the word of the Lord the heavens were made,
>> their starry host by the breath of his mouth.
> He gathers the waters of the sea into jars;
>> he puts the deep into storehouses.
> Let all the earth fear the Lord;
>> let all the people of the world revere him.
> For he spoke, and it came to be;
>> he commanded, and it stood firm.
>
> (Ps 33:4-9)

The word of the Lord is faithful and true. He is close to his people. By his word the heavens were made. He spoke and it came to be. God looks on his people and creation. The psalmist expresses his hope in God who is the Lord and creator of all.

> We wait in hope for the Lord;
>> he is our help and our shield.
> In him our hearts rejoice,
>> for we trust in his holy name.
> May your unfailing love be with us, Lord,
>> even as we put our hope in you.
>
> (Ps 33:20-22)

It is God who is the source and sustainer of life.

> If it were his intention
>> and he withdrew his spirit and breath,
> all humanity would perish together
>> and mankind would return to the dust.
>
> (Job 34:14-15)

Ps 104 is another psalm that praises the beauty of creation. The psalmist celebrates the sheer magnificence of all that God has made. After listing the many wonders, climaxing in human life itself, the psalmist speaks in amazement:

> How many are your works, Lord!
> > In wisdom you made them all;
> > the earth is full of your creatures.
>
> (Ps 104:24)

Then he goes on to praise who keeps all things in being. God is not remote from his creation or those who love him. God is active in sustaining everything that lives and breathes on the planet. He does so through the Spirit:

> All creatures look to you
> > to give them their food at the proper time.
> When you give it to them,
> > they gather it up;
> when you open your hand,
> > they are satisfied with good things.
> When you hide your face,
> > they are terrified;
> when you take away their breath,
> > they die and return to the dust.
> When you send your Spirit,
> > they are created,
> > and you renew the face of the ground.
>
> (Ps 104:27-30)

God through his Spirit is provider and sustainer. Jesus says that it is God himself who clothes the grass of the field and adorns the lilies with their beauty. It is God himself who feeds the ravens and knows when a sparrow falls to the earth (Matt 6:25-34). It God cares for these how much more will he care for his children.

> "The Lord is righteous in all his ways
> > and loving toward all he has made."
>
> (Ps 145:17)

The Holy Spirit is active also in empowering certain people for special deeds. We see this in the prophetic books when the prophet is called.

Micah says:

> But as for me, I am filled with power,
> with the Spirit of the Lord,
> and with justice and might,
> to declare to Jacob his transgression,
> to Israel his sin.
>
> (Micah 3:8)

In the Book of Judges he empowers people like Othniel (Judges 3:9-11), Ehud (Judges 3:11-29) and finally Samson (Judges 13 – 16). In Isaiah he empowers the messiah with his Spirit:

> A shoot will come up from the stump of Jesse;
>   from his roots a Branch will bear fruit.
> The Spirit of the Lord will rest on him—
>   the Spirit of wisdom and of understanding,
>   the Spirit of counsel and of might,
>   the Spirit of the knowledge and fear of the Lord—
> and he will delight in the fear of the Lord.
> He will not judge by what he sees with his eyes,
>   or decide by what he hears with his ears;
> but with righteousness he will judge the needy,
>   with justice he will give decisions for the poor of the earth.
> He will strike the earth with the rod of his mouth;
>   with the breath of his lips he will slay the wicked.
> Righteousness will be his belt
>   and faithfulness the sash around his waist.
>
> (Isa 11:1-5)

The Book of Isaiah shows God's faithfulness to faithless Jerusalem. He receives his commission in chapter 6. This call took place at a crucial time in Judah's history (6:1). He is called in the Temple. He is purged of his impiety by the Seraph. In chapter 11 Isaiah looks forward to an ideal future. God is faithful to his promise through a descendent of Jesse, the father of David. The saviour king will be empowered by the Spirit. This will be marked by an ideal time marked by the taming of wild animals

(11:6-8). This future will come when all people live in accord with God's ways. The absence of this knowledge of the Lord is the reason for alienation from God and his consequent judgement (1:3; 5:13; 6:10). This age has not yet come to be. As we will see in Romans the creation groans until the new heaven and the new earth come to be (Rom 8:22-25).

Later Judaism:
Judah came under Greek influence during the Seleucid period. There was interaction between Jewish culture and Greek culture. This created its own tensions. Chrysippus, an early Stoic, assumed "that the whole world is united by a pneuma which wholly pervades it and keeps it together" (On Mixture). Lucilius Balbus claimed that "the world order is maintained in unison by a divine and pervading spirit" (On the Nature of the Gods, 2.19). the human soul is a fragment of the cosmic soul.

Seneca (+41BC), the ancient author and Stoic, wrote of the human spirit:

> "We do not need to uplift our hands towards heaven, or to beg the keeper of a temple to let us approach this idol's ear, as if in this way our prayers were more likely to be heard. God is near you, he is with you, he is within you. This is what I mean, Lucilius: a holy spirit indwells within us [sacer intra nos spiritus sedet], one who marks our good and bad deeds, and is our guardian. As we treat this spirit, so are we treated."

The person who fulfills the Stoic ideal of being unterrified in the face of dangers, untouched by desires, does so by virtue of a spirit that, while abiding within, remains allied with its heavenly origin:

> "When a soul rises superior to other souls, when it passes through every experience as if it were of small account, when it smiles at our fears and at our prayers, it is stirred by a force from heaven.... Therefore, a great part of it abides

in that place from whence it came down to earth... the great and hallowed soul, which has come down in order that we may have a nearer knowledge of divinity, does indeed associate with us, but still cleaves to its origin..."

All of this led to the development of 'pneuma' in the Alexandrian writers. The Book of Wisdom came from this milieu. He takes the inbreathing of God (Gen 2:7) to a new level. He speaks of "the one who God breathed into him an energising soul and implanted a living Spirit" (Wisdom 15:11).

In 9:17 we read: "Who has learned your counsel, unless you have given wisdom and sent your Holy Spirit from on high?". Paul takes this up in 1 Cor 2:6-15. V. 10-13 is almost a direct quotation of this passage. The Holy Spirit inspires the study of Law and is the core of true wisdom and holiness.

At this time the intertestamental writers wrote of a Messianic figure who would bring salvation to God's people. We see this in the Psalms of Solomon. God will provide a hero who will restore his people: "God will make him mighty by means of his Holy Spirit and wise by the Spirit of understanding" (Ps Solomon 17:42). He will shepherd his flock (Ps Sol 14:45) and lead them (v. 46).

There was a Jewish sect founded at Qumran in protest against the High Priest and the politics of Jerusalem. John the Baptist is sometimes said to be part of the sect. The Dead Sea Scrolls were discovered there in 1947 and many more were found over the years. In these scrolls we see that the Holy Spirit inspires both the scriptures and prophecy. For example, 1 QS 3:7-8 (The Manual of Discipline) suggests this when it comments on Neh 9:30: "You warned them by your spirit through the prophets. Yet they would not listen". The same document comments on Zech 7:12: "the words that the Lord of Hosts had sent by his Spirit through the former prophets." 1 QS 9:11 speaks of the priestly messiah of Aaron and the kingly messiah of Israel. The Book of Jubilees is an ancient Jewish text. It claimed to present the history of the division of the days of the Law, of the events of the years, the year-weeks and the jubilees of the world, as revealed to Moses. Jubilees 31:13 recounts "And the Spirit of prophecy came down into his mouth". Jubilees 25:14 and 31:12 speak of 'the Spirit of prophecy'. This forms the background for Luke's idea: Schweizer spoke of the "typically Jewish idea that the Spirit is the Spirit of prophecy" in the context of the background to the Gospel of Luke.[7]

> In the sixth month of Elizabeth's pregnancy, God sent the angel Gabriel to Nazareth, a town in Galilee, to a virgin pledged to be married to a man named Joseph, a descendant of David. The virgin's name was Mary. The angel went to her and said, "Greetings, you who are highly favored! The Lord is with you."
> Mary was greatly troubled at his words and wondered what kind of greeting this might be. But the angel said to her, "Do not be afraid, Mary; you have found favor with God. You will conceive and give birth to a son, and you are to call him Jesus. He will be great and will be called the Son of the Most High. The Lord God will give him the throne of his father David, and he will reign over Jacob's descendants forever; his kingdom will never end."
> "How will this be," Mary asked the angel, "since I am a virgin?"
> The angel answered, "The Holy Spirit will come on you, and the power of the Most High will overshadow you. So the holy one to be born will be called the Son of God. Even Elizabeth your relative is going to have a child in her old age, and she who was said to be unable to conceive is in her sixth month. For no word from God will ever fail."
> "I am the Lord's servant," Mary answered. "May your word to me be fulfilled." Then the angel left her.
> (Luke 1:26-38)

Another important thinker of this time was Philo of Alexandria (c. 20 BCE – c. 50 CE). He represented the Alexandrian Jews in a delegation

---

[7] Eduard Schweizer, "Pneuma, pneumatikos, pneō, empneō, pnoē, ekpneō, theopneustos: E.II. Luke and Acts," in TDNT, 6.404-15, here 407.

to the Roman Emperor Caligula following strife between the Alexandrian Jewish and Greek communities. He was a leading writer of the Hellenistic Jewish community in Alexandria, Egypt, and he wrote in Greek. Philo regards the Spirit as inspiring the scriptures (On the Life of Moses, 1:175, 1.277, On the Virtues 217-219). The prophet can be completely overcome by the Spirit.

In all these works and others of this period the Spirit is personal and radiates God's presence. Erik Sjöberg writes: "There are many instances of the Spirit speaking, crying, admonishing, sorrowing, weeping, rejoicing, comforting".[8] We see an echo of this in The Letter to the Ephesians 4:30-32: "Do not grieve the Holy Spirit of God, by whom you were sealed for the day of redemption."

Another idea that began to develop at this time was the 'Shekinah'. This is not a Biblical word. It's root is in the Hebrew for tent (š-k-n in Hebrew). It is the presence of God himself. Israel's God is one who suffers and lives with Israel. "He lifted them up and carried them all the days of old" (Isa 63:9). He binds himself so closely to Israel that he becomes one in heart and soul with her. Israel's exile is God's exile. Israel's sufferings are God's sufferings: "In all their afflictions he was afflicted" (Is 63:8f), "I am with him in trouble" (Ps 91:15). The knowledge of God's suffering with them was Israel's consolation, especially when their suffering seemed hopeless. This consoles us today. The Midrash says "And the Holy One, Blessed is He, said to the children of Israel: When I saw that you left my dwelling palce, I left it also so that I might return home with you"; "When a human being suffers torment, what does the Shekinah say: My head is heavy, my arm is heavy". Ps 23:4 also speaks of the Shekinah's consoling presence and companionship "in the valley of the shadow of death."[9]

God loves his creation and is bound to us in love. He is the 'lover of life', his eternal Spirit is in all things, as their vital force. God is present in all his creatures and is himself the immanent mystery. The Holy Spirit

---

[8] Erik Sjöberg, Pneuma etc. CIII, Ruach in Palestinian Judaism, in TDNT 6:375-89.

[9] see Jürgen Moltmann, The Spirit of Life: A Universal Affirmation (London: 1992), p. 49f.

is the efficacious presence of God himself. The idea of the Shekinah lets us see this. The Spirit is God's empathy, his feeling identification with what he loves. He indwells us. He suffers with the suffering. "God removes his impassibility and becomes able to suffer because he is willing to love" (Moltmann, 51). God waits for our love. "As you did it to one of the least of my brethren, you did it to me" (Matt 25:40). In the Gospel of John we read: "The Word became flesh and made his dwelling place among us" (Jn 1:14). The Greek for 'made his dwelling place among us' could be translated as 'pitched his tent among us' – the idea of the Shekinah again.

The Christ of the Spirit:
The Holy Spirit is part of the tortured life of Jesus, the one rejected and crucified. In the early chapters of Matthew and Luke we see the action of the Holy Spirit even before Jesus was born. Luke gives us an account of the annunciation to Mary as we saw:

> In the sixth month of Elizabeth's pregnancy, God sent the angel Gabriel to Nazareth, a town in Galilee, to a virgin pledged to be married to a man named Joseph, a descendant of David. The virgin's name was Mary. The angel went to her and said, "Greetings, you who are highly favored! The Lord is with you."
>
> Mary was greatly troubled at his words and wondered what kind of greeting this might be. But the angel said to her, "Do not be afraid, Mary; you have found favor with God. You will conceive and give birth to a son, and you are to call him Jesus. He will be great and will be called the Son of the Most High. The Lord God will give him the throne of his father David, and he will reign over Jacob's descendants forever; his kingdom will never end."
>
> "How will this be," Mary asked the angel, "since I am a virgin?"
>
> The angel answered, "The Holy Spirit will come on you, and the power of the Most High will overshadow you. So the holy one to be born will be called the Son of God. Even

Elizabeth your relative is going to have a child in her old age, and she who was said to be unable to conceive is in her sixth month. For no word from God will ever fail."

"I am the Lord's servant," Mary answered. "May your word to me be fulfilled." Then the angel left her.

(Luke 1:26-38)

The same Spirit that hovered over the waters now overshadows Mary, a new thing is happening here. Mary is afraid at what the angel's greeting could mean but she abandons herself to God's will. The Holy Spirit tells her child will be holy – He is with her.

In the next scene Mary visits her cousin Elizabeth who is now pregnant with John the Baptist. Elizabeth is filled with the Holy Spirit. We read:

At that time Mary got ready and hurried to a town in the hill country of Judea, where she entered Zechariah's home and greeted Elizabeth. When Elizabeth heard Mary's greeting, the baby leaped in her womb, and Elizabeth was filled with the Holy Spirit. In a loud voice she exclaimed: "Blessed are you among women, and blessed is the child you will bear! But why am I so favored, that the mother of my Lord should come to me? As soon as the sound of your greeting reached my ears, the baby in my womb leaped for joy. Blessed is she who has believed that the Lord would fulfill his promises to her!"

(Luke 1:39-45)

Filled with the Holy Spirit she exclaims (ane-phōnēsim) in joy that Mary is blessed. The two women share their joy. This reminds us of the joy expressed in the Book of Chronicles where worship is full of joy. The people gathered with music and singing and they "raised a sound with trumpets and cymbals and instruments of song... And the house was filled a cloud of the Lord's glory (2 Chron 5:13). So now here Elizabeth is filled with the Holy Spirit and cries out in joy to welcome Mary. The child in Elizabeth's womb skipped with joy in the whole scene.

After the birth of Jesus we see that the way of Jesus is through suffering. This, too, is a part of his life. Joseph and Mary bring the child Jesus to the Temple. There they meet a man called Simeon:

> Moved by the Spirit, he went into the temple courts. When the parents brought in the child Jesus to do for him what the custom of the Law required, 28 Simeon took him in his arms and praised God, saying:
> "Sovereign Lord, as you have promised,
>   you may now dismiss[a] your servant in peace.
> For my eyes have seen your salvation,
> which you have prepared in the sight of all nations:
> a light for revelation to the Gentiles,
>   and the glory of your people Israel."
> The child's father and mother marveled at what was said about him. Then Simeon blessed them and said to Mary, his mother: "This child is destined to cause the falling and rising of many in Israel, and to be a sign that will be spoken against, so that the thoughts of many hearts will be revealed. And a sword will pierce your own soul too."
> (Luke 2:27-35)

Simeon's words remind us of the hope expressed in Isaiah 40 – 55. Simeon waited for God to come among us for the consolation of Israel. All the characters in Luke's account are not as great as the Jewish kings or the Roman occupiers. They are inconspicuous in terms of power but they are faithful in prayer. He warns that the chosen one will suffer and a sword will pierce Mary's heart.

> At that time Jesus came from Nazareth in Galilee and was baptized by John in the Jordan. Just as Jesus was coming up out of the water, he saw heaven being torn open and the Spirit descending on him like a dove. And a voice came from heaven: "You are my Son, whom I love; with you I am well pleased."
> At once the Spirit sent him out into the wilderness, and he was in the wilderness forty days, being tempted by Satan. He was with the wild animals, and angels attended him.
> (Mark 1:9-13)

Mark here tells us of the beginning of Jesus's ministry. Here the Spirit is at work again. The opening words "You are my Son" recall Psalm 2:7 where God addresses the King of Israel at his enthronement. These words show us God's endorsement of Jesus as his messiah, his anointed king. The closing words: "with you I am well pleased", pick up God's address to the inspired servant of Isaiah 42:1: "here is my servant whom I uphold, my chosen, in whom my soul delights. I have put my Spirit upon him: he will bring forth justice to the nations." Yet Isaiah's servant would be hated and murdered (Isaiah 52:13 - 52:12). Jesus too will be rejected but he will overcome death. Jesus would eventually pray during his mission (see Luke 6:12; 5:16; Matthew 14:23). He would pray in agony in Gethsemane where he "threw himself on the ground, and prayed that if it were possible, the hour might pass from him" (Mark 14:32-35).

After the Baptism the Spirit 'drove' Jesus out into the desert. This is a very strong statement. Hemingway used to speak of the "iceberg" principle in his writing. He would use sparse terms but underneath the surface there was a lot going on. It's the same with Mark. Jesus was compelled to go out into the desert and pray. He was tempted but came through. "He was with the wild beasts". This peace with all creation recalls the messianic-king prophecy of Isaiah in chapter 11. There we read:

> The wolf will live with the lamb,
>   the leopard will lie down with the goat,
> the calf and the lion and the yearling[a] together;
>   and a little child will lead them.
> The cow will feed with the bear,
>   their young will lie down together,
>   and the lion will eat straw like the ox.
> The infant will play near the cobra's den,
>   and the young child will put its hand into the viper's nest.
> They will neither harm nor destroy
>   on all my holy mountain,
> for the earth will be filled with the knowledge of the Lord
>   as the waters cover the sea.
>   (Isaiah 11:6-9)

Jesus is doing something new but he is ultimately rejected and crucified, but he shows love is stronger than death. The fullness of this new world has not yet come to be fully but we live in hope that in time it will. We are in the in-between times.

Jesus in his time did not linger when he heard the voice telling him of God's delight in him. His faith was tested and he had to learn what God's calling involved. He had a long road to travel. This is important for us to remember. We cannot stay in a state of blissful contemplation all the time. We have to face the tests of the reality of life.

In the Gospel of Luke Jesus left the desert with a clarity in his mind of his vocation – Luke tells us: "Then Jesus, filled with the power of the Spirit, returned to Galilee ... and began to teach" (Luke 4:14f). The Spirit was involved in Jesus's suffering and suffered with him. The Spirit "directs towards the Father the Sacrifice of the Son, bringing it into the divine reality of the Trinitarian communion", says St. John Paul in his encyclical "Dominum et Vivificantem" 11,41 (1986). As St. Paul says, God was in Christ reconciling the world to himself (2 Cor 5:19).

The indwelling of the Spirit in Jesus brings the divine life to fruition in Jesus. The Spirit makes Jesus 'the kingdom of God in person' (see Moltmann, p. 61). In the Spirit Jesus drives out demons and heals the sick. In the power of the Spirit he receives sinners. The power of the Spirit is given to him for others: for the sick, the poor, sinners, the dying.

Jesus's prayer in Gethsemane (see Mark 14:32-42) addresses God as 'Abba, dear Father'. Jesus experiences God's hiddenness. What began with the Baptism ends with the forsakenness of the Cross. Jesus asked those with him: "Watch and pray that you may not enter into temptation" (Mk 14:38). He feels the agony of the hour. His passion has begun. His passion ends with his cry of abandonment on the Cross: "With a loud cry Jesus breathed his last" (Mark 15:37). The divine Spirit was present in Jesus when he said: "Not my will, but thine, be done" (14:36). This surrender is now complete. In his death and resurrection Jesus brings the Spirit of God into the God forsaken world, "who intercedes for us with sighs too deep for words" (Rom 8:26). Christ's death and his resurrection are one. The Spirit's involvement in Jesus's passion and death allows us to discover a future beyond his death. "...in fact Christ has been raised from the dead, the firstfruits of those who have fallen asleep. For as by a man came death, by a man has also comes the resurrection of the dead. For as in Adam all die, so also in Christ shall all be made alive. But each in his own order: Christ the first fruits, then at his coming those who belong to Christ" (1 Cor 15:20-23). This Spirit lives in us: "Do you not know that you are God's temple and that God's Spirit dwells in you?" (1 Cor 3:16) and later Paul says again: "...do you not know that your body is a temple of the Holy Spirit within you, which you have from God and that you are not your own" (1 Cor 6:19). He tells us: "whoever is united with the Lord is one with him in spirit" (1 Cor 6:17). God's indwelling is commonly experienced as God prompting us to action and prayer. To enter this world of the Spirit, Teresa of Avila tells us "Imagine that the Lord himself is at your side and see how lovingly and how humbly he is teaching you" (Way of Perfection, chapter 26, p. 173)10 and she later says not to be worried about elaborate meditations or be worried about progress: "but only look at Him.. He is only waiting for us to look at Him... If you want Him you will find Him." (Way of Perfection, chapter 26, p. 174). Here Teresa echoes Hebrews 12:2f:

> "...fixing our eyes on Jesus, the pioneer and perfecter of faith. For the joy set before him he endured the cross, scorning its shame, and sat down at the right hand of the throne of God. Consider him who endured such opposition from sinners, so that you will not grow weary and lose heart."
> (Hebrews 12:2-3)

Hans Urs Von Balthasar reflects on the work of the Holy Spirit in the resurrection:

> The Resurrection of the dead Son is consistently ascribed to the action of the Father, and in the closest possible connexion with the Resurrection there is presented to us the

---
[10] Teresa of Avila, The Collected Works of St. Teresa of Avila, Vol. 2 (ICS Publications: 1980).

> outpouring of the divine Spirit. Only because 'God has sent the Spirit of his Son into our hearts' (Galatians 4:6) does the objective event become something that touches our own existence.... [I]t is in the strength of the Spirit of God, his pneuma, that the Resurrection of Jesus Christ is accomplished, as Romans 8, 11 and I Peter 3, 18 indicate. In this powerful, transfiguring action of his Spirit, God shows himself so much, and so definitively, the God who raises the dead that participial or relative forms—'he who raised Christ Jesus from the dead' (Romans 8, 11; II Corinthians 4, 14; Galatians 1,1; Ephesians 1, 20; Colossians 2, 12)—become, as J. Schniewind once remarked, God's 'honorific names'.[11]

Later on he says:

> Paul's contribution here was decisive in that, for him, all the problems concerning the lapse of time between the Resurrection and the sending of the Spirit fall away, since he sees the two events in the closest possible unity. We have already noted that the Father raises the Son by his Spirit (Romans 8, 11), and that the terms *dynamis* [power], *doxa* [glory], and *pneuma* [spirit], which alternate as principles of resurrection, are to a considerable degree interchangeable. But the Spirit is not only the instrument of the Resurrection. He is also the milieu in which the Resurrection takes place: *zōopoiēstheis de pneumati*, 'he was made alive in the Spirit' (I Peter 3, 18); *edikaiōthē en pneumati*, 'he was vindicated in the Spirit', (1 Timothy 3, 16; cf. Romans 1, 4). This milieu is not, however, one which Christ enters as into an environment strange to him. Rather is it an inheritance that belongs to him, since he is beforehand, as 'second Adam', the *pneuma zōopoioun*, 'life-giving Spirit' (I Corinthians 15, 45); rises again as *sōma pneumatikon*, 'a spiritual body' (I Corinthians 15, 44);

---

[11] These quotes are from Mysterium Paschale found in Eugene Rogers Jr. (ed.), The Holy Spirit: Classic and Contemporary Readings (Oxford: 2009), p. 205-207.

and is wholly identified with the realm of the Spirit ('The Lord is the Spirit', II Corinthians 3, 17). Whoever wishes to live in the Lord must live in the Spirit and by him (Galatians 5, 16, 22 and 25). John puts into words the same idea when he makes the earthly Jesus one to whom the Father gives the Spirit 'without measure' (John 3, 34) and (as the true 'rock in the desert') the dispenser *par excellence* of water and the Spirit (7, 38). Yet the rock must first be struck by the lance of the Passion before he can pour out, with his blood, this water (and that Spirit) which, before his glorification is only promised (7, 39; 4, 10 and 14), but which afterwards is both the foundation and the testimony—in the unity of the Spirit with the water and the blood—of the faith of the Church (I John 5, 6ff; John 3, 5 and 8). When Jesus on the Cross gives over his pneuma, he also, doubtless, breathes forth the Spirit who is sent on mission, 'given without measure' (*pneuma aiōnion*, Hebrews 9, 14),—the Spirit whom the Father, in raising Jesus, returns to him as in the highest possible manner personally his own, but who is henceforth also the divine Spirit, identical with *dynamis* and *doxa* and now made known openly to the world (Romans 1, 4).

This explains why for Paul, as for the author of the Acts of the Apostles, and indeed 'for the witness of all the New Testament writers', the action of the Holy Spirit, manifesting himself in the Church, remains the real proof of Christ's risen being. For that Resurrection was nothing less than Christ's taking possession of God's Spirit and power, access to which he had promised to those who believe in him. Luke for his part provides for the Church, aware as she is of her living possession of the Spirit, a central moment of a cultic kind, and one capable of being dated—namely, the event of Pentecost. Such possession of the Spirit is expressed not only in the continuation of the 'signs and wonders' on whose basis Jesus had been 'attested. . . by God' (Acts 2, 22), but also in the inner dispositions of the community: its prayer, its living faith, its brotherliness of common life, concern for the needy and so forth. Last but not least to be mentioned among these indices of the ownership of the Spirit comes: being found worthy to share in the sufferings of Christ, something only possible through the inner incorporation of believers into the realm of Christ and the Spirit.

The decisive revelation of the mystery of the Trinity is not, therefore, something which precedes the *Mysterium Paschale* [paschal mystery] itself.

In the Acts of the Apostles Jesus promises that after he leaves "you will receive power when the Holy Spirit comes on you and you will be my witness in Jerusalem…" (Acts 1:8). They returned to the upper room where they remained in prayer "along with the women and Mary the mother of Jesus, and with his brothers" (Acts 1:14). Then we read:

> When the day of Pentecost came, they were all together in one place. Suddenly a sound like the blowing of a violent wind came from heaven and filled the whole house where they were sitting. They saw what seemed to be tongues of fire that separated and came to rest on each of them. All of them were filled with the Holy Spirit and began to speak in other tongues as the Spirit enabled them.
> (Acts 2:1-4)

Pentēkostē (which we translate as Pentecost) is the Greek name for the feast of weeks (Shavuot). Luke speaks of the Pentecost event and that evokes the revelation to Moses on Mount Sinai. The twelve are like the twelve tribes gathered at Sinai. The fire recalls the appearance of God (theophany) on Sinai. The tongues symbolise the reality of God's presence. The apostles go out and preach. Luke tells us:

> No, this is what was spoken by the prophet Joel:
> "'In the last days, God says,
>   I will pour out my Spirit on all people.
> Your sons and daughters will prophesy,
>   your young men will see visions,
>   your old men will dream dreams.

> Even on my servants, both men and women,
>> I will pour out my Spirit in those days,
>> and they will prophesy.
> I will show wonders in the heavens above
>> and signs on the earth below,
>> blood and fire and billows of smoke.
> The sun will be turned to darkness
>> and the moon to blood
> before the coming of the great and glorious day of the Lord.
> And everyone who calls
>> on the name of the Lord will be saved.'
>
> (Acts 2:16-21)

Here Peter quotes Joel 3:1-5, joining it with a crucial phrase from the Greek version of Isaiah 2:2 ("in the last days"). He is saying in effect that what has been happening in Jerusalem is the fulfillment of these end-time prophecies. The Spirit is now available to all. This outpouring of the Spirit on the community is a sign of the end-times. It is also a sign of the resurrection and enthronement of Jesus. This is the Spirit we pray for. John of the Cross says in 'The Spiritual Canticle' (39.3.4): "The Holy Spirit raises the soul most sublimely with his divine breath... that she may breathe in God the same breath of love that the Father breathes in the Son and the Son in the Father."

Abandonment and Hope:
Matthew's Gospel shows in many places the Holy Spirit working through Jesus. In 12:9-14 he heals on the Sabbath; in 12:15-21 he heals the crowds – He is the anointed servant of Isaiah 42. There are many other instances of the Spirit at work. Yet in our age we think of the Spirit, if we ever think of the Spirit, as strangely silent. Man feel a sense of abandonment. In so many of the wars afflicting our world we see endless cruelty. Human beings see themselves as the apex of creation. Yet the savagery with which people kill and torture others show us we have no cause for pride. Animals don't do to other animals what human beings do against each other. The cruelty of the world can leave us feeling helpless and hopeless. Abuse of children and vulnerable people causes many to struggle through life.

Jacques Ellul (+1994) was one who battled with these thoughts. He was a French philosopher, sociologist, lay theologian and professor. He was called a Christian anarchist. He lectured at the University of Bordeaux. He was an eminent layman of the Reformed Church of France. He worked against the Nazis during World War II. In his work 'Hope in Time of Abandonment'[12] he shares with readers the darkest forebodings of human beings, but also his own struggle to emerge from despair to a stronger level of Christian faith and hope. A lack of hope is an issue in personal life and social relationships. We see violent terrorism, environmental degradation. Ellul suggest our world feels an age of abandonment. God seems far from the broader culture of our world and its institutions. The world is experiencing the silence of God. We live in an age of suspicion of which Marx, Nietzsche and Freud are the primary progenitors (pp. 48-54). Ellul says we have to get to the end of our illusory hope before we can rediscover authentic hope. The French title of Ellul's book was 'Forgotten Hope'. Hope can be found again in waiting (wakeful, persistent expectation), prayer (wrestling with God, demanding he speaks again) and realism (the reality of our world). Hope liberates and revitalises us. Perfection comes only at the End. We have to live with imperfection in the meantime.

Ellul emphasises the individual person. He follows Kierkegaard in this (p. 149f). In the crowd we become invisible. Ellul believes it is by the Holy Spirit that our ears are opened to God's word (p. 140). In translating 1 Kings 19:2 he uses Chouraqui's translation. He translates 'qol demama daqqa' as 'the fading murmur of silence' (p. 107). This is where Elijah recognises God's presence. God is lover but in our world love is not loved. In humble prayer we can rediscover this love and give some to our lives. This will allow us to enter the conflicts of our world. We are not machines but human beings. St. Teresa of Avila tells us it is by prayer we enter the Interior mansions.

One such person who placed herself before the word of God and prayed humbly was Thérèse of Lisieux (+1897). When she was nine years of age she experienced a severe illness but she saw Our Lady smile on her

---

[12] Jacques Ellul, Hope in Time of Abandonment (New York: 1973).

and she was cured. She felt the call to religious life. She was in a hurry to join – perhaps she had an intimation that she had not long for her mission. In November 1887 she went on pilgrimage to Rome and asked Pope Leo XIII to allow her enter Carmel. He told her to be patient. Eventually Thérèse overcame all obstacles and entered the Carmel at Lisieux at an early age. The incarnation is an ongoing historical event. We find our identity in coming to know Jesus and who we are in God's eyes. Von Balthasar says of Jesus: "Christ desires oneness; he would like to live in you and commingle his breath with your breathing.... He seeks trust, intimacy; He is a beggar for your love."[13] Thérèse, moved by the Holy Spirit, understood this in the depths of her being. She gave herself to love.

Herbert McCabe pointed out that Jesus was sent by God to be human and love. This is what led to his suffering. He says:

> "The mission of Jesus from the Father is not the mission to be crucified; what the Father wished is that Jesus should be human.
> ...And this is what Jesus sees as a command laid on him by his Father in heaven; the obedience of Jesus to his Father is to be totally, completely human. This is his obedience, an expression of his love for the Father; the fact that to be human means to be crucified is not something that the Father has directly planned but what we have arranged. We have made a world in which there is no way of being human that does not involve suffering."[14]

In 1890 Thérèse discovered the suffering servant of Isaiah 52:13 – 53:12. She saw how Jesus's suffering and ours can be used by God to heal his people. In this poem we read:

> He grew up before him like a tender shoot,
>   and like a root out of dry ground.

---

[13] Hans Urs Von Balthasar, The Heart of the World (San Francisco: 1979), p. 120f.
[14] Herbert McCabe, O.P., God Matters (New York: 1987), p. 93.

> He had no beauty or majesty to attract us to him,
>   nothing in his appearance that we should desire him.
> He was despised and rejected by mankind,
>   a man of suffering, and familiar with pain.
> Like one from whom people hide their faces
>   he was despised, and we held him in low esteem.
> Surely he took up our pain
>   and bore our suffering,
> yet we considered him punished by God,
>   stricken by him, and afflicted.
> But he was pierced for our transgressions,
>   he was crushed for our iniquities;
> the punishment that brought us peace was on him,
>   and by his wounds we are healed.
> We all, like sheep, have gone astray,
>   each of us has turned to our own way;
> and the Lord has laid on him
>   the iniquity of us all.
>
> (Isaiah 53:2-6)

The Servant took our pain and bore our suffering. Thérèse saw this in Jesus and in love she wished to share his suffering with him. In this way she would give expression to her love.

Thérèse sought to find a vocation that would express this love. She read St. Paul in 1 Cor 13:

> "Though I command languages both human and angelic -- if I speak without love, I am no more than a gong booming or a cymbal clashing.
> And though I have the power of prophecy, to penetrate all mysteries and knowledge, and though I have all the faith necessary to move mountains -- if I am without love, I am nothing.
> Though I should give away to the poor all that I possess, and even give up my body to be burned -- if I am without love, it will do me no good whatever."
>
> (I Cor 13:1-3)

and finally

> "As it is, these remain: faith, hope and love, the three of them; and the greatest of them is love."
>
> (1 Cor 13:13)

When she found the words "Love is the most perfect way" she realised she had discovered her vocation.

> "At last my mind was at rest... CHARITY gave me the key to my vocation. I understood that the Church had a body made up of different members, the most necessary and most noble of all could not be lacking, and so I understood that the Church had a heart, and that this heart was BURNING WITH LOVE. I understood that it was LOVE ALONE that made the Church's members act, and that if love ever became extinct, apostles would not preach the Gospel, martyrs would refuse to shed their blood. I understood that LOVE CONTAINED ALL VOCATIONS, THAT LOVE WAS EVERYTHING, THAT IT EMBRACED ALL TIME AND ALL PLACES. IN A WORD, THAT IT IS ETERNAL!
> Then, in the excess of my ecstatic joy, I cried out: O Jesus, my love, at last I have found my vocation. MY VOCATION IS LOVE!
> Yes, I have found my place in the Church and it is you, O my God, who have given me this place – in the heart of the Church, my mother, I shall be LOVE. Thus I shall be everything – and thus my dream will be fulfilled!!!
>
> (Ms B, 3v°)

Jesus is a beggar for our love. His brothers and sisters are also beggars for love. By loving Thérèse gave herself to loving those who needed love. The Holy Spirit gives many gifts for the building up of people (see 1 Cor 12-14). Love is the greatest of all and in a world of loneliness the most needed. The Holy Spirit is love and Thérèse longed to embody this love in herself. Her prayer reached beyond Carmel and touched many.

Many who came to her found healing. She continued her work after her death. In coming to know her many came to know love and healing. Her love would lead her to live the suffering servant vocation:

> He was oppressed and afflicted,
> > yet he did not open his mouth;
> he was led like a lamb to the slaughter,
> > and as a sheep before its shearers is silent,
> > so he did not open his mouth.
> By oppression and judgment he was taken away.
> > Yet who of his generation protested?
> For he was cut off from the land of the living;
> > for the transgression of my people he was punished.
> He was assigned a grave with the wicked,
> > and with the rich in his death,
> though he had done no violence,
> > nor was any deceit in his mouth.
> Yet it was the Lord's will to crush him and cause him to suffer,
> > and though the Lord makes his life an offering for sin,
> he will see his offspring and prolong his days,
> > and the will of the Lord will prosper in his hand.
> After he has suffered,
> > he will see the light of life and be satisfied;
> by his knowledge my righteous servant will justify many,
> > and he will bear their iniquities.
> Therefore I will give him a portion among the great,
> > and he will divide the spoils with the strong,
> because he poured out his life unto death,
> > and was numbered with the transgressors.
> For he bore the sin of many,
> > and made intercession for the transgressors.
> > > > > (Isaiah 53:7-12)

She was one in suffering with her beloved and many who came to know her found peace. As St. Paul says: "Death was at work in us but life in you" (2 Cor 4:12). Thérèse suffered mentally, physically and spiritually in the last eighteen months of her life. She was in deep communion with the suffering, lonely Jesus. She brought love to that place. She says: "O my Jesus, I love you... I recall that the smallest act of PURE LOVE is of more value... than all other works together" (Ms B SV°). Here she quotes St. John of the Cross, Spiritual Canticle, 29.2. Writing to her cousin Marie Guerin in 1890 she shows her recognition that Jesus needs our love. She says: "Consider Jesus, make him loved by souls... Jesus is sick [with love] and we must state that this sickness is healed only by love! ...Marie, really give your heart to Jesus. He is thirsty for it. He is hungry for it. Your heart, that is what he longs for..." (LT109). She tells us of her giving herself to this love:

> "Abandonment alone
> brings me into your arms, O Jesus.
> It alone makes me live
> The life of the elect"
> (Poem 5, stanza 7)

In another poem of 1896, entitled "How I want to love", she says:

> "It's your love, Jesus, that I crave.
> It's your love that has to transform me.
> Put in my heart your consuming flame
> And I'll be able to bless you and love you."
> (PN41)

Thérèse was also moved by reading the following passages: "Whoever is a little one, let him come to me" (Proverbs 9:4) and "As a mother caresses her child, so I will comfort you" (Isa 66:12-13). This is the language Thérèse uses to express an attitude of total surrender to God's love and mercy. She told her sister Marie of the unlimited confidence she had in her heart (LT 197). She embraces her littleness. Jesus will meet us there and he will transform us into flames of love. "It is confidence and nothing but confidence that must lead us to love." In a letter to her sister in 1897 she says: "let us esteem ourselves as little souls whom God must sustain at each moment... YES, it suffices to humble oneself, to bear with one's imperfections. That is real sanctity!"

(LT 243). God comes to us when we are weak and loves us then. As St. Paul said: "when I am weak I am strong" (2 Cor 12:10). God loves us in Jesus by the power of the Holy Spirit and the Spirit transforms us into flames of love. This is not a closed relationship. In loving we draw others into this circle of love. This is what Thérèse did and continues to do.

We have to place ourselves before the word (and Word) of God. He comes to us in unexpected ways. We have to be open and pray always. In the story of Elijah we see how he did this. It was in the gentle breeze or whisper that God was present.

> The Lord said, "Go out and stand on the mountain in the presence of the Lord, for the Lord is about to pass by."
> Then a great and powerful wind tore the mountains apart and shattered the rocks before the Lord, but the Lord was not in the wind. After the wind there was an earthquake, but the Lord was not in the earthquake. After the earthquake came a fire, but the Lord was not in the fire. And after the fire came a gentle whisper. When Elijah heard it, he pulled his cloak over his face and went out and stood at the mouth of the cave.
>
> (1 Kings 19:11-13)

Chapter 3

Where is Love?

"God is Love" (1 Jn 4:8). This is a famous part of the First Letter of John. In my experience more effort has gone into analysing the meaning of the text than in praying it. "The paralysis of analysis". Reading Abraham Joshua Heschel (+1972) helped me re-focus and appreciate the inner meaning of the text more. Heschel was a Polish American rabbi. He was professor of Jewish mysticism at the Jewish Theological Seminary of America. He was also important in the civil rights movement and in Vatican II. He was involved in the formation of the document Nostra Aetate which dealt with the relationships between the Jewish people and the Church.

One of his most famous works was 'The Prophets'.[1] He emphasises God's concern for the human being. "Prophecy is the voice that God has lent to the silent agony, a voice to the plundered poor, to the profaned riches of the world. It is a form of living, a crossing point of God and man. God is raging in the prophet's words" (page xiii). Heschel sees the Hebrew prophets as receivers of the "Divine Pathos". God is with the poor and broken and suffers in them. In his view, prophets do not speak for God as much as they remind their audience of God's voice for the voiceless, the poor and oppressed.

The prophet doesn't enter the world of matter and form, of definitions and demonstrations, he instead speaks about widows and orphans. The words of Amos echo down through the centuries:

> Hear this, you who trample upon the needy,
> And bring the poor of the land to an end,
> Saying: When will the new moon be over
> That we may sell grain?
> And the Sabbath,

---

[1] Abraham J. Heschel, The Prophets (Philadelphia: 1962).

> That we may offer wheat for sale,
> That we may make the ephah small and the shekel great,
> And deal deceitfully with false balances,
> That we may buy the poor for silver,
> And the needy for a pair of sandals,
> And sell the refuse of the wheat?
> – Amos 8:4-6 (Prophets, p. 3)

We have become accustomed to injustice, cruelty. To us a single act of injustice is slight. To the prophet it is a disaster. When we read the Gospel of Matthew we hear Jesus say: "...to the extent you did it to the least of these my brethren, you did it to me" (Matt 25:40).

Everyday we see manifestations of hypocrisy, cruelty, falsehood, outrage, violence. We rarely grow indignant or overly excited. To the prophets even a minor injustice assumes cosmic proportions: Heschel, again, quotes Amos and Jeremiah.

> The Lord has sworn by the pride of Jacob:
> Surely I will never forget any of their deeds.
> Shall not the land tremble on this account,
> And everyone mourn who dwells in it,
> And all of it rise like the Nile,
> Be tossed about and sink again, like the Nile of Egypt?
> (Amos 8:7-8)

and then he quotes Jeremiah:

> Be appalled, O heavens, at this,
> Be shocked, be utterly desolate,
> says the Lord.
> For my people have committed two evils:
> They have forsaken me,
> The fountain of living waters,
> And hewed out cisterns for themselves,
> Broken cisterns,
> That can hold no water.
> (Jeremiah 2:12-13)

The prophet is sensitive to evil and cruelty. We lack this sensitivity in our world. Ours is an age where we have forgotten how to pray, how to cry and ultimately how to love. War is raged with ferocity and slaughter, while peoples are in danger of being exterminated. The prophet in his time tried to wake people up from their indifference. Amos spoke of the indifference of people:

> They drink wine in bowls,
> And anoint themselves with the finest oils,
> But they are not grieved over the ruin of Joseph!
> (Amos 6:6)

The prophet is one who feels fiercely. God has thrust a burden on his soul. He feels God's pain at the cruelties we inflict on each other. He feels with God's heart. He feels the groaning of God's Spirit in agony. He discloses a divine pathos. The pages of the prophetic writings in the Bible are filled with echoes of divine love and disappointment, mercy and indignation (Amos 6:8; Jer 5:9, 51:14) (The Prophets, p. 28f). The divine pathos impacts every aspect of the prophet's being. The task of the prophet is to convey the word of God. The fundamental experience of the prophet is "a fellowship with the feelings of God, a sympathy with the divine pathos, a communion with the divine consciousness, which comes through the prophet's reflection of, or participation in, the divine pathos" (Prophets, p. 32). The prophet hears God's voice and feels his heart. God's heart is full of love and is broken every minute. The prophet bears a heavy burden.

Our life becomes meaningful when we serve some end beyond ourselves. We each have a mission, a vocation from God. We are needed by God to bring his healing to a broken world. Our quest for meaning is a quest for ultimate relationship and belonging. Heschel shows us the struggles of the human heart.

> "The ideals we strive after, the values we try to fulfill, have they any significance in the realm of natural processes? The sun spends its rays upon the just and the wicked, upon flowers and snakes alike. The heart beats normally within

> those who torture and kill. Is all goodness and striving for veracity but a fiction of the mind to which nothing corresponds in reality? Where are the spirit's values valid? Within the inner life of man? But the spirit is a stranger in the soul. A demand such as "love thy neighbour as thyself" is not at home in the self.
>
> We have in common a terrible loneliness. Day after day a question goes up desperately in our minds: Are we alone in the wilderness of the self, alone in this silent universe, of which we are a part, and in which we feel at the same time like strangers?"[2]

The prophets remind us of our indifference. It is when we surrender to God that we find acceptance, forgiveness and the fact we are called by him. By being who God has called us to be we bring his healing into the world. God cares for us with a passionate love. We can become his co-workers in bringing that love into the world. We see this giving of different gifts for different roles in the community:

> There are diversities of gifts, but the same Spirit. There are differences of ministries, but the same Lord. And there are diversities of activities, but it is the same God who works all in all. But the manifestation of the Spirit is given to each one for the profit of all: for to one is given the word of wisdom through the Spirit, to another the word of knowledge through the same Spirit, to another faith by the same Spirit, to another gifts of headings by the same Spirit.
> (1 Cor 12:4-9)

When we reach out to another we reach out to God. "Kindness to the poor is a loan to the Lord…" (Proverbs 19:17).

Heschel lost his family in the Holocaust. He had received an invitation to teach abroad a week before the Nazis invaded Poland. He described himself with the words from the prophet as a "branch plucked from the

---

[2] Abraham Joshua Heschel, God in Search of Man: A Philosophy of Judaism (New York: 1955), p. 101f.

fire" (Zech 3:2). His writing was his prophetic witness to our being called to be truly human – to once again become people of the Spirit. He wrote for a Jewish audience but the effect of his work went far beyond Judaism. He became an important voice in interfaith dialogue. He was an important voice in the Second Vatican Council.

It was by the Holy Spirit that the prophets were led into the heart of God and wrote of what they found. It was the same Spirit that led Heschel to help us see and hear what the prophets said. The scriptures also speak of the tenderness of God. He is very vulnerable and is a God of care and concern. It is by prayer that we discover this God and let him work in us: Francis of Assisi entered this world and his influence spread to a generation. It continues to fascinate down to this day. David Bowie (+2016) spoke of Assisi and is time there. He said "I'd like to live in Assisi, it's like being in heaven."[3] He went on to say that he loved Italy. He would have liked to live in Assisi and get closer to Giotto. Giotto painted the frescoes that showed St. Francis's life in the Basilica of San Francesco in Assisi. Bowie prayed every morning.

Prayer is an awakening to the fact that the fulfillment of my life lies in God. God delights in his creation and loves each of us with an infinite, tender love. Prayer is God's desire to give me life in the Spirit, to breathe in me, to be the Spirit of my life and to draw me into the fulness of life. When I pray I become part of the intimacy of God's life. The Spirit of God draws me into the circle of love between the Father and Son. This intimacy of prayer was at the heart of the life of Saint Francis. He told his followers to have, above all things, the Spirit of the Lord and his holy manner of working, to pray always and to have a pure heart. The first biographer of St. Francis described Francis as "living prayer". Celano writes:

> "Thus he would direct all his attention and affection toward the one thing he asked of the Lord, not so much praying as becoming totally prayer."
> (2 Celano in Francis of Assisi - Early Documents II, p. 310)

---

[3] see Giuseppe Bellini, La Stampa, 16 September 1995.

This ultimately shapes our lives and the way we live. It shapes what we become in the world we live in. The Flame of Love was enkindled in his heart. Flames and fire have always been symbols of divinity and of God's action in the world. John of the Cross wrote "The Living Flame of Love" as a poem that celebrates the flame of love that is the Holy Spirit. In the fourth stanza the Holy Spirit is described through the image of "sweet breathing". Breathing is a sign of life. The Holy Spirit is thus a living flame which breathes into the soul pure love and provokes a response of love. The entire poem is written as an intense moment of prayer to the Holy Spirit, expressing love, wonderment and delight. In the prologue he speaks of the analogy of the log of wood, the fire. It is transformed by the fire. It is the same with us – we have to grow in the Spirit (Prologue, 4).

In stanza 2 we read:

> O sweet cautery,
> O delightful wound!
> O gentle hand! O delicate touch
> that tastes of eternal life
> and pays every debt!
> in killing you changed death to life.

The soul is wounded with love. He speaks of the case of Saint Francis. He says:

> Let us return to the work of that seraph, for he truly inflicts a sore, and wounds inwardly in the spirit. Thus, if God sometimes permits an effect to extend to the bodily senses in the fashion in which it existed interiorly, the wound and sore appear outwardly, as happened when the seraph wounded St. Francis. When his soul was wounded with love by the five wounds, their effect extended to the body, and these wounds were impressed on the body, which was wounded just as his soul was wounded with love.

Saint Francis came to know the true love of God in the Holy Spirit. He saw this love revealed in Jesus especially in his death and resurrection.

He was one in love with Jesus in the Spirit and bore the marks of the crucifixion on his body. The flame of divine love filled St. Francis so entirely that "it seemed that the whole universe is a sea of love in which it is swallowed" (The Flame of Love 2:10). Francis had learned universal compassion and this is what drew so many to him. He led people to healing and peace. Clare of Assisi (+1253) followed St. Francis and always pointed to Jesus in whom we find our peace. She too was filled with infinite love.[4] Both knew the heart of God and brought others to know and experience that heart. Their whole lives show an alternative way of life is possible even now. Charles de Foucauld (+1916) is another such person. We will meet him later.

Carlo Rocchetta has written much about "the tenderness of God".[5] The Biblical word in consideration is Rahûm and is close to the word rhm. It refers to tenderness in the most inner part or being of the person. It is used in 1 Kings 3:26 where a mother worries about her child with compassion. The verb rāham means to have pity on, to have compassion for. This comes from an intense love. God is the one full of compassion. In isaiah we read:

> Though the mountains be shaken
>   and the hills be removed,
> yet my unfailing love for you will not be shaken
>   nor my covenant of peace be removed,"
>   says the Lord, who has compassion on you.
>
>   (Isa 54:10)

The word for 'compassion' here is mə-ra-ḥă-mêḵ, a variation on the word rhm. The root for the verb rahum comes from the word for compassion. The Book of Deuteronomy reminds us: "For the Lord your God is a merciful God; he will not abandon or destroy you or forget the covenant with your ancestors, which he confirmed to them by oath." (Deut 4:31).

---

[4] see my Clare of Assisi: A Living Flame of Love (Athlone: 2013).
[5] Carlo Rocchetta, Teologia della Tenerezza: Un "Vangelo" da Riscoprire (Bologna: 2014 ed.).

The tenderness and compassion of God is often used of the love of a mother for her child. In fact it is even greater. The prophet Isaiah writes about God's feeling of compassion, tenderness and love:

> But Zion said, "The Lord has forsaken me,
>   the Lord has forgotten me."
> "Can a mother forget the baby at her breast
>   and have no compassion on the child she has borne?
> Though she may forget,
>   I will not forget you!
>
>   (Isa 49:14-15)

Psalm 103 also tells about this love of God. We read: "As a father has compassion on his children, so the Lord has compassion on those who love him" (Ps 103:3). Isaiah 54:7 says: "For a brief moment I abandoned you but I take you back with infinite tenderness" (rachamim). Psalm 25:6 and Ps 40:11 say: "Remember, Lord, your mercy" (rahum). In the prophet Hosea we read: "I will cure their infidelities, I will love them from the heart" (Hos 14:4). Compassion and infinite love are part of God's very being. This is the love that Francis and Clare lived in by the power of the Holy Spirit.

It is God's dream that this love will usher in a new age, the time of the 'New Heaven' and the 'New Earth'. In Rev 21 we have a description of this world.

> Then I saw "a new heaven and a new earth," for the first heaven and the first earth had passed away, and there was no longer any sea. I saw the Holy City, the new Jerusalem, coming down out of heaven from God, prepared as a bride beautifully dressed for her husband. And I heard a loud voice from the throne saying, "Look! God's dwelling place is now among the people, and he will dwell with them. They will be his people, and God himself will be with them and be their God. 'He will wipe every tear from their eyes. There will be no more death' or mourning or crying or pain, for the old order of things has passed away."

He who was seated on the throne said, "I am making everything new!" Then he said, "Write this down, for these words are trustworthy and true."

He said to me: "It is done. I am the Alpha and the Omega, the Beginning and the End. To the thirsty I will give water without cost from the spring of the water of life.
(Rev 21:1-6)

We share in God's dream when we share in his love and bring that love to bear in our lives. It is in this way that darkness is overcome and a new order is ushered in. In 'The Brothers Karamazov' we read:

"Love all God's creation, both the whole and every grain of sand. Love every leaf, every ray of light. Love the animals, love the plants, love each separate thing. If thou love each thing thou wilt perceive the mystery of God in all; and when once thou perceive this, thou wilt thenceforward grow every day to a fuller understanding of it: until thou come at last to love the whole world with a love that will then be all-embracing and universal."
– The Monk Zossima, chapter 41 in The Brothers Karamazov by Fyodor Dostoevsky

It is in the Spirit and through him we learn this universal love. Jesus Christ is the Word incarnate. In him we find our true identity. In mapping out the spiritual journey Clare indicated the goal of union with God is imitation (2 LAg 20). St. Francis meditated on the Crucified and became one with him even to the point, as we saw, to carrying the wounds of Christ on his body. He looked "unto Jesus" (Heb 12:2). St. Bonaventure tells us:

After true love of Christ
Transformed the lover into His image,
When the forty days were over that he spent in solitude
As he had desired,
And the feast of St. Michael the Archangel
Had also arrived,

> The angelic man Francis
> Came down from the mountain,
> Bearing with him
> The likeness of the Crucified,
> Depticted not on tablets of stone or on panels of wood
> Carved by hand,
> But engraved on parts of his flesh
> By the finger of the living God.
> – Bonaventure, The Major Legend of Saint Francis

The author of the Gospel of John explores the depth of Jesus's life and its significance. We are called through the words to come into intimate communion with Jesus in the Spirit – we are called to be "oned" with him (The Cloud of Unknowing).

The Gospel of John:

> In the beginning was the Word, and the Word was with God, and the Word was God. He was in the beginning with God. All things came into being through him, and without him not one thing came into being. What has come into being in him was life, and the life was the light of all people. The light shines in the darkness, and the darkness did not overcome it.
>
> There was a man sent from God, whose name was John. He came as a witness to testify to the light, so that all might believe through him. He himself was not the light, but he came to testify to the light. The true light, which enlightens everyone, was coming into the world.
>
> He was in the world, and the world came into being through him; yet the world did not know him. He came to what was his own, and his own people did not accept him.
>
> But to all who received him, who believed in his name, he gave power to become children of God, who were born, not of blood or of the will of the flesh or of the will of man, but of God.

And the Word became flesh and lived among us, and we have seen his glory, the glory as of a father's only son, full of grace and truth. (John testified to him and cried out, "This was he of whom I said, 'He who comes after me ranks ahead of me because he was before me.'") From his fullness we have all received, grace upon grace. The law indeed was given through Moses; grace and truth came through Jesus Christ. No one has ever seen God. It is God the only Son, who is close to the Father's heart, who has made him known.
(John 1:1-18)

The phrase "In the beginning" in verse 1 echoes Genesis 1:1 and alerts the reader to the fact that a new creation is present here. The "word" (Logos)[6] is already present in the Old Testament. Logos is translated as 'word'. In Ps 33 we read:

By the word of the Lord the heavens were made,
   their starry host by the breath of his mouth.
He gathers the waters of the sea into jars;
   he puts the deep into storehouses.
Let all the earth fear the Lord;
   let all the people of the world revere him.
For he spoke, and it came to be;
   he commanded, and it stood firm.
(Ps 33:6-9)

It came to mean in the Old Testament the creative energy of God as in Genesis 1 and Isaiah 55. In Greek philosophy 'logos' means 'order', 'reason' or 'harmony'. It could mean the soul of the word. The work of the Logos is related to the work of divine Wisdom in the late Old Testament (Wisdom 7:25, 8:5, 9:1, 9:9-11 and Proverbs 8:21-31). These passages describe a feminine 'Wisdom'.

Wisdom is the co-worker and co-creator with God. What God was, the Logos was in John. In the Logos was light, and that was the light of all

---

[6] see my A Love Supreme (London: 2019) where I consider the meaning of Logos in more detail, p. 100-107.

humankind. The Logos was with God and was God. Jesus was the 'Logos made flesh'.

In 1:6-17 John plunges into the complexity of history and ordinary life, as the Word becomes a human being. Its culmination (1:18) tells us that no-one knows God except his one and only son. He is himself God and since he is close to the Father he has made him known.

All who accept the call to enter this intimacy in the Spirit between God and the Word become "children of God" who, as the rest of the Gospel shows, receive the Spirit that is breathed by Jesus into his disciples, leading them "into all the truth" (Jn 16:13). John the Baptist was the herald of Jesus and calls us to follow him. The intimacy of Jesus and the Father frames and introduces the drama of Jesus's life, death and resurrection and giving of the Spirit. It also shows us the drama of following Jesus in the company of his friends (Jn 21:19;22).

In Genesis 1:3 we heard the words, "Then let there be Light" and here in John we hear "In the beginning was the Word" (1:1). In the rest of the Prologue John takes further and identifies the Word with God as God's full self-expression. In the first letter of St. John we read:

> That which was from the beginning, which we have heard, which we have seen with our eyes, which we have looked at and our hands have touched—this we proclaim concerning the Word of life. The life appeared; we have seen it and testify to it, and we proclaim to you the eternal life, which was with the Father and has appeared to us. We proclaim to you what we have seen and heard, so that you also may have fellowship with us. And our fellowship is with the Father and with his Son, Jesus Christ. We write this to make our joy complete.
> (1 John 1:1-4)

As in the Gospel (1:1) the opening line speaks of the beginning referring here primarily to the revelation of Jesus in which the community has placed its faith. The Word is the Word of life, the Logos. It has become real and concrete in the person of Jesus. He was seen (Jn 1:39, 14:9, 19:35, 20:18,25) and even touched (Jn 20:27). The author and his community have seen and touched the Word of Life. He gives his testimony so that the readers may have life. Fellowship with John and his community means the mutual indwelling of the Father and the Son (Jn 17:11, 21 and 23) and this is the source of joy that he wishes his readers to experience (Jn 15:11; 17:13). The Spirit is the one who brings this about. Through him we are called to experience this indwelling and experience hope and joy. God is love (1 Jn 4:8, 16) and his Word is Love for us. This love is poured into our hearts by the Spirit given us (Rm 5:5) as St. Paul says.

In John 14 we read:

> "If you love me, keep my commands. And I will ask the Father, and he will give you another advocate to help you and be with you forever— the Spirit of truth. The world cannot accept him, because it neither sees him nor knows him. But you know him, for he lives with you and will be in you. I will not leave you as orphans; I will come to you. Before long, the world will not see me anymore, but you will see me. Because I live, you also will live. On that day you will realize that I am in my Father, and you are in me, and I am in you. Whoever has my commands and keeps them is the one who loves me. The one who loves me will be loved by my Father, and I too will love them and show myself to them."
> (John 14:15-21)

Jesus has told the disciples of his coming departure, but he promises to be with them in a new way. He will be present in the Spirit. Knowing Jesus is the same as knowing the Father. In verses 10-12 Jesus spoke of dwelling in the Father and the Father in him. Love also means knowing God as an empowering principle and surrendering to him. Jesus promises the advocate or the Paraclete. This is the fulfillment of the idea of rebirth in the Spirit that Jesus spoke of in 3:1-8. The Spirit will mean the presence of Jesus in the community (14:15-17, 25-26; 15:26-27; 16:7-11 and 12-15).

"Paraclete" was originally a legal term meaning advocate, counsellor or stand in, it fulfilled a variety of functions: teaching 14:17; prophecy 14:2-3 and 16:13-15; witness 8:7-18 and 15:26. Its origin is God (15:26 and 16:28). John's community is a Spirit filled community.

> Jesus replied, "Anyone who loves me will obey my teaching. My Father will love them, and we will come to them and make our home with them. Anyone who does not love me will not obey my teaching. These words you hear are not my own; they belong to the Father who sent me.
> "All this I have spoken while still with you. But the Advocate, the Holy Spirit, whom the Father will send in my name, will teach you all things and will remind you of everything I have said to you. Peace I leave with you; my peace I give you. I do not give to you as the world gives. Do not let your hearts be troubled and do not be afraid."
> (Jn 14:23-27)

The Holy Spirit banishes fear and the feeling of distance from God. That is why Jesus says "Do not let your hearts be troubled or afraid" (v. 27). Jesus tells the disciples he is in their hearts. This is done by the Holy Spirit. St. Teresa of Avila teaches us that the person who is entering contemplation is in the seventh mansion. This person perceives the presence of the Trinity, Father, Son and Holy Spirit.

> First of all the spirit becomes enkindled and is illumined, as it were, by a cloud of the greatest brightness. It sees these three Persons, individually, and yet, by a wonderful kind of knowledge which is given to it, the soul realises that most certainly and truly all these three Persons are one Substance and one Power and one Knowledge and one God alone; so that what we hold by faith the soul may be said here to grasp by sight, although nothing is seen by the eyes, either of the body or of the soul, for it is no ordinary vision.
> (Interior Castle, 7, chap 1)

This is the treasure that lies at the centre of a being. We are God's delight. We are his dwelling place. This communion with God is called by Teresa the Spiritual Marriage.

> "I have much more to say to you, more than you can now bear. But when he, the Spirit of truth, comes, he will guide you into all the truth. He will not speak on his own; he will speak only what he hears, and he will tell you what is yet to come. He will glorify me because it is from me that he will receive what he will make known to you. All that belongs to the Father is mine. That is why I said the Spirit will receive from me what he will make known to you."
> (John 16:12-15)

The disciples will be comforted and be joyful in the Spirit. He will remind them of what he said. The Spirit will receive from Jesus what he will give to the disciples. The Spirit is the one who will guide the disciples into all truth (John 16:13). It is the Spirit's vocation to take believers and form them into knowers and lovers of God. It is the Spirit who makes saints and the saints are witnesses to the work of the Holy Spirit. St. Paul said in Christ "are hidden all the treasures of wisdom and knowledge" (Col 2:3).

Hans Urs Von Balthasar (+1988) tells us that the Spirit makes the truth known by drawing the knower into participation in God through love. In Theo-Logic 3, he sees the chief task of the Spirit is to incorporate the knower into the life of God.[7] The Spirit leads into all truth through the union of love with God and the truth of the wounds in the hypostatic flesh of Christ – that is true God and true man (Theo-Logic 3, p. 18). Von Balthasar always saw the work of nature as a form of beauty. Now he sees creation gather around the person of Christ, causing the divine light to shine on all things and see all through God's eyes. Balthasar's Spirit is the dialogue of love between Father and Son. The Holy Spirit is the subject of divine love, "the space between Father and Son, into which the Spirit introduces us, is in a certain respect the Spirit himself"

---

[7] Hans Urs Von Balthasar, Theo-Logic 3 (San Francisco: 2000).

(Theo-Logic p. 18). St. Paul tells us that the Spirit "searches the deep things of God" (1 Cor 2:10).

Von Balthasar draws on the thought of Saint Basil when he says:

> the Spirit "wishes only to breathe through us, not to present himself to us as an object; he does not wish to be seen but to be the seeing eye of grace in us."[8]

Christ and the Spirit are intimately connected. In speaking of Christ we have to speak of the Spirit and when we speak of the Spirit we have to speak of Christ.

The Spirit deepens our faith and in many ways makes known the identity of God as love. The foundational understanding of the Spirit in Balthasar's theology is the idea of 'donum' (gift), the Spirit as the gift of love in the life of God. He is the "proof and fruit" of the love of Father and Son (Theo-Logic, p. 159). He is the object of the shared love of the Father and Son (Theo-Logic, p. 164). Balthasar quotes Richard of St. Victor's arrangement of the Spirit as both the object of the Father and Son and as the subjective object of Trinitarian love.

> When two love each other, exchanging the gift of their heart in intense longing, and love flows from the one to the other and from the other to the one and thus in each case tends in an opposite direction toward a diverse object, there is indeed love on both sides, but the partners do not yet love with each other [condilectio]. We cannot say that they love with each other until the two love a third in harmonious unity, lovingly embracing him in common [socialiter], and the affection of the two surges forth as one in the flame of love for the third.[9]

It is the Spirit as Love who knows the truth that God is Love. The Spirit's knowledge and love is the eternal grounding of all love, truth

---

[8] Basil of Caesarea, On the Holy Spirit, VIII, 40 quoted in Theo-Logic, p. 26.
[9] Richard of St. Victor, De Trinitate, p. 19, quoted in TL 2 p. 41.

and knowledge. He leads us into this love and it is by love we come to know God. Love, too, is a form of knowing.

St. John of the Cross wrote his Living Flame of Love for a widow named Ana de Peñalosa. It was the only work he wrote for a lay-person, not for religious sisters. The first verse reads:

> "O living flame of love
> that tenderly wounds my soul
> in its deepest center! Since
> now you are not oppressive,
> now consummate! if it be your will:
> tear through the veil of this sweet encounter!"

The soul feels that it is inflamed in the divine union. It is surrounded by all glory and love. It feels that from its depths will flow rivers of living water (see Jn 7:38). The flame of love is the Spirit of the bridegroom, who is the Holy Spirit (Flame 1:3). The soul comes to be united with the flame and gives out flames of love itself. He compares the soul to a log of wood immersed in fire. Eventually "the acts of the soul blaze up from the fire of love" (Flame 1:4). This is a foretaste of the new creation. The soul is wounded with the tenderness of God's love. The flame of love is a metaphor for the Holy Spirit acting on the soul. The Spirit leads to a purification and transformation in love. In this way the acts of the soul become divine. This takes place in the deepest centre of the person. The soul's centre is God (Flame 1:12). Love is the inclination, strength and power for the soul in making its way to God, for love unites it with God (Flame 1:13). It is only in the next life that this love will be perfect. The term "substance of the soul" refers to the deepest and most intimate parts of one's being. John describes the action of the living flame (the Holy Spirit) in the soul as a celebration, a feast. Having been purified it is not held back but in love can receive the one who loves us. We find our home in God. John of the Cross quotes Jesus "in my father's house are many dwelling places (mansions)" (Jn 14:2). We cannot reach the perfect state of glory in this life. The Blessed Trinity inhabits the soul. It illuminates the intellect with the Wisdom of the Son, delighting its will in the Holy Spirit, and absorbing it powerfully and mightily in the unfathomed embrace of the Father's tenderness. Paul too speaks of the indwelling of the Holy Spirit. He says: "You are the temple of the Living God" (2 Cor 6:16). Here Paul is anxious for the Corinthians to dissociate themselves from all that could take them away from Christ. As a community they constituted the spiritual temple of God in virtue of its being indwelt by the Spirit of God (1 Cor 3:16-17). In 1 Cor 6:19 Paul says "Do you not know that your body is a temple of the Holy Spirit. The Spirit is in you and is a gift from God". We have a unique dignity in the eyes of God. Another way of saying that one is moved by the Holy Spirit, according to Paul, is to say "in Christ": "Therefore if any man is in Christ, he is a new creature: old things have passed away; all things become new" (2 Cor 5:17).

St. Augustine puts the idea of the indwelling of the Holy Spirit and the Trinity beautifully. He says:

> "Late have I loved you, beauty so old and so new: late have I loved you. And see, you were within and I was in the external world and sought you there, and in my unlovely state I plunged into those lovely created things which you made. You were with me, and I was not with you. The lovely things kept me far from you, though if they did not have their existence in you, they had no existence at all. You called and cried out loud and shattered my deafness. You were radiant and resplendent, you put to flight my blindness. You were fragrant, and I drew in my breath and now pant after you. I tasted you, and I feel but hunger and thirst for you. You touched me, and I am set on fire to attain the peace which is yours."
> (St. Augustine of Hippo, Confessions)

In the world of Paul the Holy spirit is the pledge and guarantee of the world to come. In the letter to the Ephesians, which we will say belongs to the world of Paul, we read:

> In him you also, when you heard the word of truth, the gospel of your salvation, and believed in him, were sealed with the

promised Holy Spirit, who is the guarantee of our inheritance
until we acquire possession of it, to the praise of his glory.
(Ephesians 1:13, 14 ESV)

The Holy Spirit makes us certain that God will give us what he promised. In the second letter to the Corinthians Paul writes: "He has sealed us and given us the Spirit as a downpayment in our hearts" (2 Cor 1:22). The Holy Spirit is a downpayment of the new creation to come. In Christ we become a new creation (2 Cor 5:17).

Jesus's death is recounted by John in chapter 19. He says:

> Later, knowing that everything had now been finished, and so that Scripture would be fulfilled, Jesus said, "I am thirsty." A jar of wine vinegar was there, so they soaked a sponge in it, put the sponge on a stalk of the hyssop plant, and lifted it to Jesus' lips. When he had received the drink, Jesus said, "It is finished." With that, he bowed his head and gave up his spirit.
> (John 19:28-30)

Jesus exclaims "I thirst" to fulfill Ps 69:21. Sour wine is given to him on a sprig of hyssop which was used to smear the blood over the lintels before Passover (Ex 12:21-23). He then declares "It is finished". "Tetelestai" can mean finished or accomplished. He has achieved all that the Father has sent him to do (Jn 17:14) and now his mission is complete. He has truly "loved them to the end" (13:1). After his death he hands over the Spirit, signifying both his death and the release of the Spirit promised in 7:39 and 14:16-17. The new community of the "women and the Beloved Disciple" at the foot of the Cross share in his Spirit and are the bearers of the Spirit in the world. In this sense Jesus's mission is accomplished and is still being accomplished. Jesus rises from the dead by the power of the Holy Spirit. He breathes this Spirit on the disciples in the Upper Room (John 20:21-23). The Gospel means to bring us into this communion in the Spirit and live in God's Spirit in the here and now. St. Paul reminds us that here and now "we do not know how to pray as we ought, but the Spirit himself intercedes for us through wordless groans" (Rom 8:26). We have our part to play in the healing of the world and the making of the world to come, 'The New Heaven and the New Earth'. Paul says: "For the creation waits with eager longing for the revealing of the sons of God" (Rom 8:19) and later "the whole creation has been groaning together in the pains of childbirth until now" (Rom 8:22). The world we see is not the end but we live in the times of the pains of childbirth of the new order.

Symbols for the New Creation:
At this moment we are cut off from Heaven. We have stark reminders of this every day as we see the innocent butchered. There is inequality, rampant greed and selfishness. To use a metaphor, the world groans giving birth to the New Order. The New Creation is beginning even now in those in whom the Spirit indwells with the Father and the Son. One day the New Creation will come to full life.

The Book of Revelation has symbols for the New Creation. One of them is the new Jerusalem:

> Then a voice came from the throne, saying:
> "Praise our God,
>   all you his servants,
> you who fear him,
>   both great and small!"
> Then I heard what sounded like a great multitude, like the roar of rushing waters and like loud peals of thunder, shouting:
> "Hallelujah!
>   For our Lord God Almighty reigns.
> Let us rejoice and be glad
>   and give him glory!
> For the wedding of the Lamb has come,
>   and his bride has made herself ready.
> Fine linen, bright and clean,
>   was given her to wear."
> 					(Fine linen stands for the righteous
> 						acts of God's holy people.)
> 					(Rev 19:5-8)

This comes after the destruction of evil, symbolised by Babylon. The new Jerusalem is clothed with fine linen which stands for the righteous acts of God's holy people. Those who live quiet lives in union with Jesus are much more important than we imagine. They bring in the new order. Paul said in Romans "nothing will be able to separate us from the love of God that is in Christ Jesus our Lord (Rom 8:39). The image of the New Jerusalem gives us hope that this union will lead to the healing of the world. In the letter to the Ephesians St. Paul prays:

> For this reason I kneel before the Father, from whom every family in heaven and on earth derives its name. I pray that out of his glorious riches he may strengthen you with power through his Spirit in your inner being, so that Christ may dwell in your hearts through faith. And I pray that you, being rooted and established in love, may have power, together with all the Lord's holy people, to grasp how wide and long and high and deep is the love of Christ, and to know this love that surpasses knowledge—that you may be filled to the measure of all the fullness of God.
> (Ephesians 3:14-19)

This prayer is for us that we may come to know Jesus and his love and respond. In this way we help usher in the New Creation, the new Jerusalem.

Matryona's House is a novella written in 1959 by Alexander Solzhenitsyn. The narrator is a former prisoner of the Gulag and a teacher of mathematics. Matryona offers him a place to live in. She works for little pay. She is not someone the world pays a lot of attention to. She dies tragically. Her kindness had meant much to the narrator and he remarked she used to pray when she thought nobody was looking. The concluding lines read: "None of us who lived close to her perceived that she was the one righteous person without whom, as the saying goes, the village could not endure... Nor the city... Nor all our land."[10] It is through the lives of God's "little saints" like Matryona that God heals the world and ushers in the New Creation.

---

[10] Alexander Solzhenitsyn, Matryona's House and Other Stories (London: 1988), p. 47.

In Chapter 21 of Revelations the author uses the symbols of the New Heaven and the New Earth to symbolise the New Creation.

> Then I saw "a new heaven and a new earth," for the first heaven and the first earth had passed away, and there was no longer any sea. I saw the Holy City, the new Jerusalem, coming down out of heaven from God, prepared as a bride beautifully dressed for her husband. And I heard a loud voice from the throne saying, "Look! God's dwelling place is now among the people, and he will dwell with them. They will be his people, and God himself will be with them and be their God. 'He will wipe every tear from their eyes. There will be no more death' or mourning or crying or pain, for the old order of things has passed away."
> He who was seated on the throne said, "I am making everything new!" Then he said, "Write this down, for these words are trustworthy and true."
>
> (Rev 21:1-5)

This vision sees a transformation of this worldly reality. The prophets of the Old Testament used the bridal image to describe the restoration of the biblical Judah (e.g. see Isa 49:18, 52:1 and 61:10). In the prophet Ezekiel we read: "I will make them a covenant of peace... My dwelling shall be with them. I will be their God and they shall be my people" (Ezek 37:26-27). As narrated in the previous vision (Rev 20:11-15) the old order depicted by the dragon, the beasts of the land and sea, Death and Hades, have passed away. Therefore there are no more tears, no more grief. God is making all things new. The prophet Isaiah had written: "On this mountain... the Lord God will wipe away the tears form all faces" (Isa 25:7-8).

The New Heaven and the New Earth form a new Eden. We read:

> Then the angel showed me the river of the water of life, as clear as crystal, flowing from the throne of God and of the Lamb down the middle of the great street of the city. On each side of the river stood the tree of life, bearing twelve

> crops of fruit, yielding its fruit every month. And the leaves of the tree are for the healing of the nations. No longer will there be any curse. The throne of God and of the Lamb will be in the city, and his servants will serve him.
> (Rev 22:1-3)

John saw the tree of life eternally yielding good fruit. It can do so because its roots are watered by the eternal river of life. John describes all the nations being there. Humans are restored to a new state of Eden.

There is no temple in the new Jerusalem because God himself lives there among his people, all his people.

> They will see his face, and his name will be on their foreheads. There will be no more night. They will not need the light of a lamp or the light of the sun, for the Lord God will give them light. And they will reign for ever and ever.
> (Apocalypse 22:4-5)

The Book ends with a prayer for all this to come about. "Maranatha, come Lord Jesus".

> He who testifies to these things says, "Yes, I am coming soon."
> Amen. Come, Lord Jesus.
> The grace of the Lord Jesus be with God's people. Amen.
> (Rev 22:20-21)

Chapter 4

The Spirituality of Paul the Apostle

Spirituality is a word derived from Spirit. In Paul we see his thinking about being led by the Spirit. We have met Paul at different times but now we look at him in his own right. For Paul to be led by the Spirit and to be in Christ are one and the same thing. Christ and the Spirit are inseparable. They work together.

The "conversion" of Paul:
Paul began his career as a believing Pharisee. The Pharisees were a group distinguished by strict observance of the traditional and written law. Paul speaks of himself in the letter to the Philippians:

> "If someone else thinks they have reasons to put confidence in the flesh, I have more: circumcised on the eighth day, of the people of Israel, of the tribe of Benjamin, a Hebrew of Hebrews; in regard to the law, a Pharisee; as for zeal, persecuting the church; as for righteousness based on the law, faultless."
>
> (Phil 3:4b-6)

Paul was proud of his heritage. It shaped the way he looked at the Old Testament. In the Acts of the Apostles we learn that Paul "studied at the feet of Gamaliel" (Acts 22:3). Gamaliel was a famous Pharisee teacher and a grandson of the famous Rabbi Hillel. It was under his tutelage that Paul developed an expert knowledge of the Hebrew Scriptures. Paul followed all the Pharisee ways of feast-days and praying in the Temple. He consented to the killing of Stephen and was an enemy of the new movement (see Acts 7:58 - 8:2).

Paul had an encounter with the risen Christ which changed him. The Lord appeared to him in his resurrected glory (see Acts 9:1-9). His name had been Saul but is now Paul, the name we know him by. He had been an enemy of the new group. He tells us:

> For you have heard of my previous way of life in Judaism, how intensely I persecuted the church of God and tried to destroy it. I was advancing in Judaism beyond many of my own age among my people and was extremely zealous for the traditions of my fathers.
> (Gal 1:13-14)

On the road to Damascus Jesus asked him: "Saul, Saul, why do you persecute me?" (Acts 9:4). Saul asks:

> "Who are you, Lord?" Saul asked.
> "I am Jesus, whom you are persecuting," he replied. "Now get up and go into the city, and you will be told what you must do."
> (Acts 9:5-6)

Paul meets the glorified Jesus risen from the dead. The importance of the resurrection became important for Paul. He tells us:

> For what I received I passed on to you as of first importance: that Christ died for our sins according to the Scriptures, that he was buried, that he was raised on the third day according to the Scriptures, and that he appeared to Cephas, and then to the Twelve. After that, he appeared to more than five hundred of the brothers and sisters at the same time, most of whom are still living, though some have fallen asleep. Then he appeared to James, then to all the apostles, and last of all he appeared to me also, as to one abnormally born.
> (1 Cor 15:3-8)

Paul saw himself as commissioned by Jesus to preach the Gospel. He says:

> I want you to know, brothers and sisters, that the gospel I preached is not of human origin. I did not receive it from any man, nor was I taught it; rather, I received it by revelation from Jesus Christ.
>
> For you have heard of my previous way of life in Judaism, how intensely I persecuted the church of God and tried to destroy it. I was advancing in Judaism beyond many of my own age among my people and was extremely zealous for the traditions of my fathers. But when God, who set me apart from my mother's womb and called me by his grace, was pleased to reveal his Son in me so that I might preach him among the Gentiles, my immediate response was not to consult any human being.
>
> (Gal 1:11-16)

Paul enjoyed a mystical experience. In the second letter to the Corinthians he describes this mystical experience. He speaks in the third person but it is obvious he is speaking about himself.

> It is necessary to boast; nothing is to be gained by it, but I will go on to visions and revelations of the Lord. I know a person in Christ who fourteen years ago was caught up to the third heaven—whether in the body or out of the body I do not know; God knows. And I know that such a person—whether in the body or out of the body I do not know; God knows— was caught up into paradise and heard things that are not to be told, that no mortal is permitted to repeat. On behalf of such a one I will boast, but on my own behalf I will not boast, except of my weaknesses. But if I wish to boast, I will not be a fool, for I will be speaking the truth. But I refrain from it, so that no one may think better of me than what is seen in me or heard from me, even considering the exceptional character of the revelations. Therefore, to keep me from being too elated, a thorn was given me in the flesh, a messenger of Satan to torment me, to keep me from being too elated.
>
> (2 Cor 12:1-7)

Paul speaks of his journey in coming to know Jesus. He says:

> Indeed, I count everything as loss because of the surpassing worth of knowing Christ Jesus my Lord. For his sake I have suffered the loss of all things and count them as rubbish, in order that I may gain Christ and be found in him, not having a righteousness of my own that comes from the law, but that which comes through faith in Christ, the righteousness from God that depends on faith— that I may know him and the power of his resurrection, and may share his sufferings, becoming like him in his death,
>
> (Phil 3:8-10)

He regards coming to know Christ as a gain. Earlier he had spoken of his Jewish heritage. Now he speaks of "the supreme good of knowing Christ Jesus my Lord" (3:8). To be found "in him" looks forward in faith and trust to the final judgement. Those who are "in Christ" have no reason for fear (2:16).

Verses 9-11 describe the letting go of former privileges "to know the power of his resurrection" (3:10). "Resurrection" points to the present experience of Jesus the Christ even in the midst of present suffering (see 2 Cor 4:7-18; 5:17). To be "in Christ" is already to walk in the "newness of life" (Rom 6:4 cf 7:6). All of this is a gift from God not dependent on law or tradition (3:9). Here now we suffer with Christ but come to know the power of his resurrection. Christ is present to Paul by the power of the Holy Spirit and Paul is in union with Jesus the Christ, who now lives. Paul finds himself living a life where he will experience in full the resurrection of Christ. Until then he lives the life of Christ here and now. He feels in himself the fullness of Christ's love.

In the Letter to the Galatians Paul says:

> I have been crucified with Christ. It is no longer I who live, but Christ who lives in me. And the life I now live in the flesh I live by faith in the Son of God, who loved me and gave himself for me.
>
> (Galatians 2:20)

Paul and Jesus are not the same people but they are united in love by the Holy Spirit. He has come to know and love the Jesus who loved him and gave himself for Paul. For Paul his life meant getting to know Jesus and assimilating his life to his and for him. He affirms of his own life:

> "I have been crucified with Christ.
> It is no longer I who live,
> but Christ lives in me."
>
> (Gal 2:20)

Paul is in union with the crucified Christ in all his life, but this union always leads to a resurrection and this hope sustains Paul in all his trials. He knows the vitality of the resurrected Christ. He knows he is deeply loved and precious and this draws Paul to love in return. In chapter 13 of the first letter to the Corinthians Paul shares his great hymn to love. This was a text beloved of St. Thérèse of Lisieux:

> If I speak in the tongues of men and of angels, but have not love, I am a noisy gong or a clanging cymbal. And if I have prophetic powers, and understand all mysteries and all knowledge, and if I have all faith, so as to remove mountains, but have not love, I am nothing. If I give away all I have, and if I deliver up my body to be burned, but have not love, I gain nothing.
>
> Love is patient and kind; love does not envy or boast; it his not arrogant or rude. It does not insist on its own way; it is not irritable or resentful; it does not rejoice at wrongdoing, but rejoices with the truth. Love bears all things, believes all things, hopes all things, endures all things.
>
> Love never ends. As for prophecies, they will pass away; as for tongues, they will cease; as for knowledge, it will pass away. For we know in part and we prophesy in part, but when the perfect comes, the partial will pass away. When I was a child, I spoke like a child, I thought like a child, I reasoned like a child. When I became a man, I gave up childish ways. For now we see in a mirror dimly, but

then face to face. Now I know in part; then I shall know fully, even as I have been fully known.

So now faith, hope, and love abide, these three; but the greatest of these is love.

(1 Cor 13:1-13)

The love Paul describes here is the love of God revealed in Jesus and shared with us by the Spirit. Paul has just spoken of the gifts of the Spirit but if love is lacking then we have missed the mark. Love is the most important. Paul is speaking to his Corinthian audience so that they would not get proud of having the gifts. If they neglect love then their gifts are fruitless. Paul is advocating behaviour governed by love that transcends self-interest, jealousy and competitiveness that leads to strife and division. Love leads to reconciliation and unity. Love is the one thing that lasts. What Paul said to his Corinthian audience resonates with so many down through the centuries. It is as true in our time as it was with the 1st century Christian audience.

Paul and the Spirit:

The love Paul speaks of is the love of God poured into our hearts by the Spirit given us (see Romans 5:5). We hear of the Spirit in the letter to the Ephesians. There has been controversy about the authorship of Ephesians and Colossians. However they do show the influence of Paul and belong to the Pauline corpus. For now I just use "Paul" as the author without settling any debates. A seal is generally taken as a mark of identity and belonging. In the Song of Songs (8:6) the beloved asks her lover to set her "as a seal upon your heart, as a seal upon your arm: for love is strong as death, passion fierce as the grave". It was God's invitation that by praying the Gospel in Christ we were sealed as God's people by the Holy Spirit. "Paul" says that the Holy Spirit is the pledge and seal of our inheritance.

> In Christ we have also obtained an inheritance, having been destined according to the purpose of him who accomplishes all things according to his counsel and will, so that we, who were the first to set our hope on Christ, might live for the

> praise of his glory. In him you also, when you had heard the word of truth, the gospel of your salvation, and had believed in him, were marked with the seal of the promised Holy Spirit; this is the pledge of our inheritance towards redemption as God's own people, to the praise of his glory.
> (Ephesians 1:11-14)

In common usage a pledge was a downpayment, a guarantee. The Holy Spirit as God's seal both unites us to God as his and is the pledge guaranteeing the redemption of our bodies. Elsewhere Paul sees the seal as the first fruits of our salvation in Christ (Romans 8:22-23). The Spirit of God's glory is now the Spirit of Christ and is transforming us from glory to glory into the image of Christ (2 Cor 3:17-18). To be conformed to the image of Christ we should be "transformed by the renewing of your minds, so that you may discern the will of God – what is good and acceptable and perfect" (Romans 12:2). In the body of Christ: "To each is given the manifestation of the Spirit for the common good" (1 Cor 12:18,7). The Holy Spirit seals us into intimate union with God's life, where each one is special and beloved. "Therefore, if anyone is in Christ, the new creation has come: The old has gone, the new is here" (1 Cor 5:17).

The idea of new creation which we saw in the Book of the Apocalypse is also Paul's idea. The first to speak of the new order was the prophet in the Book of Isaiah.

> For, behold, I create new heavens and a new earth:
> And the former shall not be remembered, nor come into mind.
> But be glad and rejoice forever in what I create:
> For, behold, I create Jerusalem as a rejoicing,
> And her people a joy.
> I will rejoice in Jerusalem,
> And joy in my people;
> The voice of weeping shall no longer be heard in her,
> Nor the voice of crying.
> (Isa 65:17-19)

Earlier in chapters 60 and 61 the prophet spoke of the future hope of Israel as God's bride. The new Jerusalem the prophet envisions is not the city he lived in. It will be part of the new world that God will bring into existence. This is the first step in the direction of the Book of Revelations "new Jerusalem coming down out of heaven" (Rev 21:1-3). The new Jerusalem will be a joy and delight, not the feeble and forlorn city of this world. 2 Peter 3:13 reinterprets the prophet's vision of the "new heaven and a new earth".

Paul, too, has his interpretation of the end times. In 1 Cor 15 he says:

> I tell you this, brothers: flesh and blood cannot inherit the kingdom of God, nor does the perishable inherit the imperishable. Behold! I tell you a mystery. We shall not all sleep, but we shall all be changed, in a moment, in the twinkling of an eye, at the last trumpet. For the trumpet will sound, and the dead will be raised imperishable, and we shall be changed. For this perishable body must put on the imperishable, and this mortal body must put on immortality. When the perishable puts on the imperishable, and the mortal puts on immortality, then shall come to pass the saying that is written:
> "Death is swallowed up in victory."
> "O death, where is your victory?
> O death, where is your sting?"
> The sting of death is sin, and the power of sin is the law. But thanks be to God, who gives us the victory through our Lord Jesus Christ.
>
> (1 Cor 15:50-57)

How this comes about is a mystery hidden from the world (1 Cor 2:7). Paul uses apocalyptic images (e.g. suddenness, the sound of the trumpet, awaking of the dead) to describe the end-time resurrection scenario. We already saw how John in the Apocalypse described the end-time. Paul says our mortal body will be clothed in incorruptibility. We will be totally transformed. When this occurs the promise of the victory over sin and death will be fulfilled because of what God has done in Christ. We are on the way to this final victory.

The gifts of the Spirit are the enabling power by which we live. By living in the Spirit the people of God should be a blessing to all the nations. This fulfills God's promise to Abraham (Rom 3:8,14). He reminds the Corinthians the Spirit of God now dwells in them (1 Cor 3:16; 6:19).

In 2 Corinthians Paul piles up the imagery. We are confirmed into Christ, anointed, sealed and given the "arrabōn" of the Spirit in their hearts (2 Cor 1:21-22). The Spirit is the downpayment, the "arrabōn", the beginning of the salvation process which ends in the New Creation, the new Heaven and the new Earth. He is the assurance we are given now of God's victory. In the letter to the Romans Paul characterises the "true Jew" as one circumcised in the heart, "in Spirit and not in letter" (Rom 2:29). The Spirit received is experienced as liberating, motivating and enabling. In 1 Cor 12:3 the experience of inspiration is seen as the work of the Spirit. The test is the inspired confession: "Jesus is Lord" (Rom 8:15-16). It is an experience of sharing in Jesus's own sonship where we can cry "Abba, Father". This is the language Jesus used to show his intimacy with the Father (Mark 18:36). Paul uses 'abba' twice, once in Gal 4:6 and in Romans 8:15.

Paul tells us that each one is gifted to hold up the community. In 1 Cor he lists the various gifts given to members of the community.

> There are diversities of charisms, but the same Spirit. There are diversities of service, and the same Lord. There are diversities of activities, but the same God, who effects all things in everyone. To each is given the manifestation of the Spirit for the common good. To one is given a word of wisdom through the Spirit, to another a word of knowledge in accordance with the same Spirit, to another faith by the same Spirit, to another charisms of healing by the one Spirit, to another miraculous activities, to another prophecy, to another discernment of spirits, to another kinds of tongues, to another interpretation of tongues. One and the same Spirit effects all these, distributing to each as he wills. For just as the body is one and has many members and all

> the members of the body, though many, are one body, so also is Christ. For in one Spirit we were all baptised into one body, whether Jews or Greeks, whether slaves or free, and all watered with the one Spirit. For the body does not have one member but many...
>
> (1 Cor 12:4-14)

Paul uses the word "gifts" (charismata). We receive what we have as a gift. To each is given a manifestation of the Spirit. To devalue any gift is to devalue the work of the Spirit. That which is an authentic gift of the Spirit must benefit others – the gifts are not for self-glorification. Paul then carries his argument forward by means of an analogy between the church and the body. When one part hurts, all hurt. I discovered this afresh when I had cancer. The whole body was affected even though the tumour was just in one area. We are bound in a living unity with the risen Lord, which is effected through the activity and the presence of the Holy Spirit. Though we are many, we form one body.

Paul reminds us of this in the Letter to the Romans:

> For as we have many members in one body, but all the members do not have the same function, so we all are one body in Christ, and individually members of one another – having charisms which differ in accordance with the grace given to us, whether prophecy in proportion to faith, or service in service, or the one who teaches in teaching, or the one who encourages in encouraging, the one who shares with sincere concern, the one who cares with zest, the one who does acts of mercy with cheerfulness.
>
> (Romans 12:4-8)

In the Letter to the Ephesians we have another list of gifts for the good of all:

> But to each of us has been given grace in accordance with the measure of the gift of Christ... "He gave gifts to humans."... And he gave some as apostles, some as

prophets, some as evangelists, and some as pastors and teachers, to equip the saints for the work of ministry, for the upbuilding of the body of Christ...

(Ephesians 4:7-16)

The charism is the contribution the member makes for the good of all. The charism is the "manifestation of the Spirit for the common good" (1 Cor 12:7). In the different lists Paul included some human tasks and organisational roles (see Ephesians 4:7-16) as well as the more eye-catching prophecy, tongues and miracles. Each has a role to play and we should not despise anyone or their gift. The greatest gift of all is love (1 Cor 13). Love never fails (1 Cor 13:8) but we do! Paul's words remain a challenge to us and hold up before us the ideal we strive after. All the other gifts eventually fail but love remains. God reveals his love in Jesus and this love is poured into our hearts by the Holy Spirit (see Rom 5:5). In the Letter to the Romans Paul tells us:

> Who then is the one who condemns? No one. Christ Jesus who died—more than that, who was raised to life—is at the right hand of God and is also interceding for us. Who shall separate us from the love of Christ? Shall trouble or hardship or persecution or famine or nakedness or danger or sword? As it is written:
> "For your sake we face death all day long;
>   we are considered as sheep to be slaughtered."
> No, in all these things we are more than conquerors through him who loved us. For I am convinced that neither death nor life, neither angels nor demons, neither the present nor the future, nor any powers, neither height nor depth, nor anything else in all creation, will be able to separate us from the love of God that is in Christ Jesus our Lord.
>
> (Romans 8:34-39)

God never withdraws his love from us. We have to grow in the Spirit to know this. As we grow in this love we bring God's love to reign in our lives and it is in this way God brings in the new Heaven and the new Earth:

> We know that the whole creation has been groaning as in the pains of childbirth right up to the present time. Not only so, but we ourselves, who have the firstfruits of the Spirit, groan inwardly as we wait eagerly for our adoption to sonship, the redemption of our bodies. For in this hope we were saved. But hope that is seen is no hope at all. Who hopes for what they already have? But if we hope for what we do not yet have, we wait for it patiently.
> (Romans 8:22-25)

The entire world of creation is waiting for the world of God's redeemed people before it reaches its fullness in the new creation. As Paul said in 1 Cor 5:17: "Therefore if anyone is in Christ, they are a new creation". God works through us to heal the world. This is not the way we think about things. Paul shows us the way God thinks of us. We saw this expressed in a different way in the Book of the Apocalypse.

In this heady new world of the Spirit we can find it difficult to come to terms with and pray. There are many trials, vicissitudes, questions and confusion in our lives, but we are not alone. Paul goes on:

> In the same way, the Spirit helps us in our weakness. We do not know what we ought to pray for, but the Spirit himself intercedes for us through wordless groans. And he who searches our hearts knows the mind of the Spirit, because the Spirit intercedes for God's people in accordance with the will of God.
> And we know that in all things God works for the good of those who love him, who have been called according to his purpose.
> (Romans 8:26-28)

We experience now the foretaste of what is to come. We are already children of God. We received the spirit of adoption and we can call God 'Abba, Father' (8:15). The Spirit is with us in our inability to cope and he is with us when we pray, and intercedes to God with us when we cannot find the words. In God we find that "all things work for the good of those who love him" (8:28). In the Spirit God is always at work in us. So often we do not think in these terms. That is why we need to soak in the words of Paul and we see ourselves as God sees us.

Andy Warhol did a series of painting Campbell's soup cans. Warhol could not explain what he meant. He allowed the viewer make up his or her mind. Warhol had worked in advertising in the 1950's. When he did his series on Campbell's soup he used his advertising know-how, but in reverse. He made the soup cans look lifeless and flat. He was incredibly shy. So his lack of comment allows the viewer to think for themselves. No two alike will think the same thing. This is my reflection on Andy's soup cans. These are the icons of today – the world of glossy supermarkets and marketing. In the Gospel of Matthew we read: "For the mouth speaks what the heart is full of" (Matt 12:34). We become what we meditate on in life. That is why we need to embrace what Paul tells us: "We are the beloved of God".

Chapter 5

Into the Desert

Charles de Foucauld was canonised by Pope Francis on 15th May 2022. He was an apostle to the poor and was devoted to living the "hidden life" of Jesus, that is, the ordinary life of poor men and women. He was devoted to interreligious dialogue. His life was one marked by transformation: he served as a soldier, then as an explorer, then he had a conversion experience and he became a monk. Then finally he became a hermit in the desert, spending most of his time serving the Tuareg people of Algeria. He looked after the poor and outcasts in his hermitage. He witnessed to his faith through his quiet example, living with deep prayer. He was friend and "brother" to all. At the end of his encyclical "Fratelli Tutti" (2020) Pope Francis wrote:

> "Yet I would like to conclude by mentioning another person of deep faith who, drawing upon his intense experience of God, made a journey of transformation towards feeling a brother to all. I am speaking of Blessed Charles de Foucauld. Blessed Charles directed his ideal of total surrender to God towards an identification with the poor, abandoned in the depths of the African desert. In that setting, he expressed his desire to feel himself a brother to every human being, and asked a friend to "pray to God that I truly be the brother of all". [287] He wanted to be, in the end, "the universal brother". Yet only by identifying with the least did he come at last to be the brother of all. May God inspire that dream in each one of us. Amen." (Fratelli tutti, 286-287)

Charles, towards the end of his life, had the face of an ascetic which was illuminated by an inner light, a supernatural understanding and an infinite kindness. He was filled with the Holy Spirit. He would say regularly the following prayer:

> Love of the Father,
> Love of the Son,

Spirit of life, breath of God,
With your presence fill my heart,
Abide in me, life and light.
>   *Jean-Jacques Antier*
>   *Charles de Foucauld*

He devoted himself to following Jesus and he would lose his life living in obscurity. He shared the fate of so many in our world who die alone. He prayed as one of them. He prayed for those who feel or felt abandoned.

Who was Charles de Foucauld?

His mother was Élisabeth Beaudet de Morlet. She had a melancholy disposition. She saw life as a long ordeal intended to make one worthy of Heaven. His father was Viscount Édouard de Foucauld. He was an assistant inspector of forestry in Strasbourg. He married Élisabeth in 1855; he married for love. It was an attraction of opposites. Élisabeth was introverted and modest, melancholy and tender. Édouard had frittered away his youth, with drunken parties. He had little education and no money.

Édouard and Élisabeth's first child died at an early age. Then Charles was born on September 15th, 1858, at 3 Place de Broglie in the house where Rouget de Lisle had first sang the "Marseillaise". Marie was born three years later who was delicate and anxious.

Unexpectedly Édouard experienced a severe psychotic breakdown and left his family. Élisabeth died in childbirth and Édouard followed her six months later. These tragic events affected the two children severely. Next to die was Édouard's mother who looked after the children when the parents died. She died of a heart attack. Charles kept all his sadness locked up in his heart. The only expression his grief could get was unexpected tantrums when he was in school.

In 1868 he met someone who would become a great influence in his life. This was his older cousin, Marie Moitessier (Marie de Bondy as she was called after her marriage). Marie had a winning personality and a deep piety, as well as a strong will. She was eight years older than Charles but at the same time they became great friends. In 1872 when Charles made his first communion Marie gave him a copy of Bossuet's "Elevations on the

Mysteries", a book that was to have a great influence on his later conversion. A lot was to happen between 1872 and 1886 in Charles's life.

After the death of their paternal grandmother, Charles and his sister were taken in by their maternal grandparents, Colonel Beaudet de Morlet and his wife who lived in Strasbourg. De Morlet, who had been an engineering officer, provided his grandchildren with an affectionate upbringing. Charles wrote of him:

> "My grandfather whose beautiful intelligence I admired, whose infinite tenderness surrounded my childhood and youth with an atmosphere of love, the warmth of which I still feel emotionally."[1]

Charles pursued his studies at Saint-Arbogast episcopal school and went to Strasbourg high school in 1868. He was introverted and very often ill. He received private tuition at home. De Morlet loved him deeply but did not know how to cope with Charles' disturbed nature. He spend the summer of 1868 with his aunt, Inès Moitessier, who felt responsible for her nephew. Her daughter was Marie Moitessier who became friendly with Charles.

In 1870 the de Morlet family fled the Franco-Prussian War and found refuge in Bern. Following the French defeat, the family moved to Nancy in 1871. Charles had four years of secular high school left. Jules Duvaux was a teacher of his and he bonded with fellow student Gabriel Tourdes. He developed patriotic sentiments and a hatred for Germany. His first communion took place on 28th April 1872 and his confirmation at the hands of Monsignor Joseph-Alfred Foulon in Nancy followed afterwards.

In October 1873, whilst in a Rhetoric class, he began to distance himself from the faith. He later said: "The philosophers are all in discord. I spent twelve years not denying and believing nothing, despairing of the truth, not even believing in God. No proof to me seemed evident."[2] This led to a time of great distress and unease. He found himself to be "all selfishness, all impiousness, all evil desire, I was all through distraught". (Six, Charles de Foucauld). On 11th April 1878 his cousin Marie married Olivier de Bondy. A few months later Charles obtained his baccalauréat.

---

[1] Jean-François Six, Charles de Foucauld autrement. (Paris: 2008).
[2] Letter from Charles de Foucauld to Henri de Castries, 14 August 1901.

Charles felt as if he had gone mad.[3] He went to the Jesuits in Paris where strict discipline grated on him. He wanted a military career. At the time he abandoned all religious practice completely. He then returned to Nancy where he studied at home. During his reading with Gabriel Tourdes he wanted to enjoy "that which is pleasant to the mind and body".[4] The two friends discovered the works of Aristotle, Voltaire, Erasmus, Rabelais and Laurence Sterne.

In June 1876, he applied for entry to the Saint-Cyr Military Academy. At this time his grandfather died and left Charles a substantial inheritance. Charles was given to excess in everything. He earned the nickname "Piggy" from his friends in the regiment. After his graduation from Saint-Cyr, 333rd out of a class of 386, he was posted to the 4th Regiment of Chasseurs d'Afrique in Algeria.

When Charles looked back at this time in his life he wrote:

> "From then on, I am in the night, I have nothing left: I no longer see God, nor men: there is only me, and I am my sensuality, gluttony, laziness, pride, shameful passions; it is absolute selfishness in the darkness and the mud."[5]

But he came to see that he was still held by the mercy of God, even in the midst of the "night" and "mud" of this period. He said:

> "In this state of death, you still preserved me: you preserved in my soul the memories of the past, the esteem of the good, the attachment, sleeping like a fire under the ashes but still existing, to certain beautiful and pious souls, respect for the Catholic religion and for the religious: all faith had disappeared, but respect and esteem were intact... You preserved in me a disgust for vice and ugliness. I was doing the right things but I neither approved nor loved him. You made me feel a deep sadness, a painful emptiness, a sadness that I never felt until then."
>
> (La Dernière Place, p. 113)

---

[3] Jean Jacques Antier, Charles de Foucauld (San Francisco: 2022), p. 31.
[4] Alain Vircondelet, Charles de Foucauld: "Comme un agneau parmi les loups" (Monaco: 1997).
[5] Charles de Foucauld, La Dernière Place (Nouvelle Cité: 2002), p. 164f.

To cover up his loneliness Charles looked for love everywhere – he lived a life of excess but this couldn't lift the deep loneliness he felt inside. His time in the army was tempestuous and ill disciplined as before. His regiment was sent to Algeria in 1880 and he conspired to bring his mistress, Mimi, with him. This was forbidden. He refused to send her home. How like Charles! He was cashiered and came back to France where he continued to waste his fortune on wine, women and parties.

In 1881 an insurrection broke out in Algeria and Charles's old regiment was called into action. Charles abandoned his mistress and sought to be reinstated. We hear no more word of Mimi. Her feelings and hopes were dismissed. Charles was called back. In war he showed himself a good soldier and leader. He won the respect of all. After the insurrection he resigned from the army. He had come to love Africa and the vast expanse of the desert. He had a sense of the divine in nature, but he still felt a distance from God. He marveled at the prayers of the people and was deeply moved by their sincerity. He felt this was lacking in his life. He began to pray that God would somehow show himself so he could believe too.

Charles resolved to explore the unknown parts of Morocco. He spent a year of preparation in Algiers, studying Arabic and reading about North Africa. During the period 1883-1885, disguised as a Jewish peddler and with a Jewish merchant he wandered through Morocco mapping out the terrain. He received hospitality in many Muslim centres and he was touched to see their faith and the active way they practiced it. Charles was now really on a journey of the Spirit. He would write later that God would use all that he had felt had kept him away from God (La Dernière Place, p. 114). At this time Charles fell in love with Marie-Marguerite Titre. She was a Protestant. With Charles returned to Paris his family felt it wasn't a good match. Charles acquiesced and broke off the engagement. This was cruel for Marie-Marguerite.

Charles published his work on his travels in North Africa. He was admitted to "La Société de Geographie" in Paris by Oscar Mac Carthy. He was presented with a medal by the president of the Society - Ferdinand de Lesseps. He became a celebrity. However, there was a deep ache in his heart. He thought of the time when he contemplated the infinite number of stars. He hoped for a sign from God to ease his loneliness.

His Conversion:

Charles met again his cousin Marie de Bondy. He re-read the book she had given him on his first communion. He had many spiritual conversations with her. His prayer now was: "O God, if you exist, make yourself known to me." He wrestled with his doubts and the emptiness inside.

In Marie he saw a noble and gentle soul which spoke to him of a higher order (La Dernière Place, p. 117). She told him of an Abbé Huvelin who was her confessor. He worked in Église Saint-Augustin. He had a successful academic career but his health suffered in later life. He suffered mentally and physically but he was a sought-out confessor for both the rich and the poor. Charles began to attend classes given by Abbé Huvelin. Charles felt envious of his cousin Marie because she had the light of faith but he could not find that light.

Towards the end of October in 1886 he approached Abbé Huvelin and told him of his spiritual quest and how he had not found God. Huvelin asked him to enter his confessional. Charles did and confessed his life. He felt an enormous relief and an inpouring of love. He felt the love and mercy of God. God's love had been poured into his heart "through the Holy Spirit who has been given to us" (Rom 5:5). He had been fasting and so he received Holy Communion. He told his friend Henri de Castries that as soon as he understood there is a God he had to give himself totally to this God (Antier, p. 104). His vocation would go through many twists and turns.

Charles's family thought it would be good now if he married but Charles had other ideas. He was a man of extremes. Now that he had come to know God he had to give his all to God. He wrote to his friend Henri de Castries that he now sought a religious order to join but did not know which one. "The Gospels showed me that the first commandment is to love God with all one's heart and enclose everything in that love. The first effect of love is imitation." (Antier, p. 105). At this stage the imitation that appealed to him was humility, poverty and hiddenness. He said: "Thus I should imitate the hidden life of the poor and humble workman of Nazareth" (Antier, p. 105). Father Huvelin was now his spiritual director and advised him not to rush into religious life. He had to find his feet first in his new life. In late 1888 and early 1889 he began a pilgrimage to the Holy Land. He visited Jerusalem, Bethlehem and Nazareth. He also began reading Teresa of Avila at this time, something he would do for the rest of his life. After this Charles made up his mind to join the Trappists. They were also known as the "Order of Reformed Cistercians of Our Lady of La Trappe". They were named after "La Trappe Abbey", the monastery from which the group came. The movement had begun with the reforms that Armand Jean le Bouthillier de Rancé had begun in 1664 of the Cistercians. This evolved into the Trappist group. They became an independent group in 1892.

At first Charles joined the monastery of Notre-Dames des Neiges, in the Ardèche region of France. He did not believe that this was severe enough for him. He changed to a poorer monastery that this monastery had set up in Cheikhlé near Akbés in Syria in order to continue his formation under the guidance of Dom Polycarpe. In February 1892 he made his profession and took his vows. His name in religion was Brother Marie-Albéric. Here he developed a great love for the poor. He remembered Jesus's words: "Whatever you do for the least of my brothers you do for me" (Matt 25:40). Brother Marie-Albéric suffered from what was called 'consumption' at the time but he did recover. At this time he began to study theology.

It was at this time that Charles began to feel the need to found a new order to follow more closely the poverty of Jesus. He wrote to Abbé Huvelin about his dreams and hopes. He first thought of the name 'The Hermits of the Sacred Heart' and later 'The Little Brothers of Jesus'. Abbé Huvelin found his rule too taxing and would put aspirants off.

All this time Charles struggled with his Trappist vocation. He asked to leave but instead was sent to Rome to study theology. After this he met Dom Sebastien Wyart who agreed to relieve him from his vows. He was prepared for the next stage of his spiritual journey.

The Hidden Life:
Charles left for the Holy Land in 1897 and he arrived in Nazareth. There he worked for the Poor Clares as a servant. He spoke of his life there:

> "God enabled me to find what I was looking for: the imitation of what was the life of Our Lord Jesus in the very same Nazareth…"
> "In my wooden plank hut and at the foot of the Poor Clares' Tabernacle, through my days of work and my nights of prayer,

I had all that I had been looking for, so that it was clear that God had prepared this place for me."

But Charles wanted to share this life of Nazareth with other brothers. This is why he wrote the Rule of the Little Brothers.

> "I wanted to compose a very simple rule, apt to give to a few pious souls a family life around the Sacred Host."
> "My rule is so closely linked to the cult of the Holy Eucharist that it cannot be followed by a group without there being a priest among them and a tabernacle; it is only when I am a priest and there is an oratory around which we can come together, that I will be able to have a few companions."

This was a happy time in Charles's life. He devoted himself to prayer, adoration, all the time living poorly in a small shack that he asked for from the Poor Clares. Mère Marie-Ange de Saint Michel was the abbess of the Poor Clares in Nazareth. She recommended that Charles talk to her superior Mère Elizabeth de Calvarie in Jerusalem. She saw that Charles was special – she recommended that Charles become a priest. Father Huvelin agreed:

> "I went to spend a year in a convent. I studied and received Holy Orders there. I have been a priest since last June and I felt called straight away to go to the "lost sheep", to the most abandoned, the most needy, so as to fulfill the commandment of love towards them: Love others as I have loved you, this is how you will be recognised as my disciples". Knowing by experience that no people were more abandoned than the Muslims of Morocco and the Algerian Sahara, I requested and obtained permission to go to Beni Abbès, a little oasis in the Algerian Sahara on the borders of Morocco".

Bishop Bonnet had agreed to ordain Charles, seeing that he had a special vocation. Charles would be ranked among the priests of his diocese. He was actually sub-deacon ordained by Archbishop Montéty who was called in because Bishop Bonnet was ill. In 1900 Abbé Huvelin had told him to follow where the master led him. He was being led by the Holy Spirit. Charles was ordained in Viviers in 1901. Charles wrote to Marie de Bondy about the special affection he had for Bishop Bonnet:

"For me, he is still the best, the most tender and loving father. What wisdom and what strength of character."

(Antier, p. 239)

Bishop Bonnet was in favour of Charles's mission and encouraged him. He warned him there would be pitfalls in the way:

"Yes, I approve of your planned Union of Brothers and Sisters of the Sacred Heart of Jesus. But if God wants it to become a reality, how many obstacles it is going to encounter and how much suffering will be required before it wins its place in the sun of the Holy Church!"

(Antier, p. 239)

Dom Martin and Charles (now Father Charles) went back to Notre-Dame des Neiges. It was here he had prepared for his ordination. Charles spent the whole night in adoration into the morning of June 10. Then he celebrated his first Mass. Marie de Blic, his sister, was nearby. The next phase in his journey of the Spirit was near. "Go where the Spirit leads you" was the advice of Abbé Huvelin.

The Desert:
Marie de Bondy undertook all the expenses of Charles's journey and his settling in. The officers of the military posts, stationed from Algiers to Ain-Sefra, awaited him and celebrated his arrival at every station. He had been an army man and he understood them. He was persuaded by General Cauchemez to take a horse and he was escorted by a Lieutenant Huot. The region was still barely docile. Several Fathers had been massacred in the desert. At Béni-Abbès Captain Regnault awaited Charles and here Charles began his mission. He celebrated his first Mass on 1st of November, 1901. The captain built him a hermitage – an oratory, three cells and a guest room. In his early pilgrimage through Morocco he had come across a "zaouia", a muslim place of prayer and hospitality. He hoped to found a Christian place of prayer and hospitality. He hoped to form "a little family, imitating the virtues of Jesus so perfectly that all around begin to love Jesus" (12 March 1902, Lettres à Henri de Castries, p. 122).

He wished to form his confraternity of the Sacred Heart. On the back wall of his chapel he hung a canvas on which he had painted the Blessed Virgin surrounded by saints below and "above, is a full length Sacred Heart, of more or less natural height. The Sacred Heart inspires repentance with outstretched arms to embrace, to hug, to call all men and to give Himself for all, offering them His Heart." (7 January 1902, Lettres à Marie de Bondy). He saw himself as a brother to all. He was loved by the soldiers. He was kind, gentle and full of the spirit of love. This would have attracted them alone. Also they knew of his time in the army. He had been one of them. Charles was one with Jesus and "…whoever is joined to the Lord becomes one spirit with him" (1 Cor 6:17). He became a home for the indwelling Trinity and he was deeply in love with all. He had published earlier "Reconnaissance au Maroc" which was widely known. Military people came to him to discuss his findings on his trip to Morocco.

He was disturbed to find slavery still existed. He wrote to the French parliament about this. In his hermitage he welcomed all and met them with kindness and love. Many of the poor who came to him were careful not to ask too much from him. They knew he was actually very poor – so they knew not to ask too much. He shared everything he had and they came to love him. He was know as a Christian 'Marabout' – a marabout was a holy man in Islam. Mohammed told his followers to respect 'people of the book' meaning mainly Jews and Christians. It has been extended more recently to other religions. Charles became known as "Diff el Rabbi" the guest from God. This guest from God made all welcome and soon he had many people calling on him. His fame spread throughout the desert world. He was much loved. Captain Regnault said that "Khaoua Carlo is sacred". This is how Charles was known in the desert and he brought comfort and healing to all who called to him. He lived as he prayed. The Muslims thought of him as a genuine marabout.

Charles spoke of the presence of Jesus all around him. One night he read Psalm 20 and he wrote an evening prayer:

> "How sweet they are, these hours of the night! You are there, my Creator, you are in me, around me. You fill my little cell. You envelop me. All is silent outside, all is sleeping. The darkness envelops all beings, and you permit me to stay awake at your feet, so that I alone in this death of nature am living for

you. My Beloved, when all slumbers, how sweet it is to tell you that we love you, that we wish to live for you alone."[6]

He wrote to his friend, Suzanne Perret, the Lyon mystic who had offered her life for Charles and his mission:

> "In a few days I shall be going back to my cell and the solitary Tabernacle, feeling more deeply than ever that Jesus wants me to work to establish this double family [the Little Brothers and Sisters]. How? By pleading, by immolating myself, by dying, by becoming more holy, and, finally, by loving him! I beseech you to help me. Our Lord is impatient. His hidden life is not being imitated. The days we have allotted to love, to imitate, are passing by, and we do not love him, we do not imitate him, we do not redeem."

He was still the only Little Brother in the world. He prayed to Our Lady in the following words:

> "Beloved Mother, convert the Tuareg, let the Little Brothers and Sisters of Jesus come into being. May they be your faithful instruments. Unworthy creature that I am, convert me. Cherished Mother, I ask you on my knees, from the depths of my misery."

Charles did return to France a few times. The first journey was in 1909. He and Marie de Bondy had agreed to stay in contact but not to see each other again. However Marie got permission from Father Huvelin to see Charles and they did meet again. Charles also met Louis Massignon. He was a convert but was interested in Islam and the Arab world. Charles's circle of influence was ever growing.

In 1905 De Foucauld moved deeper into the Sahara. He needed more solitude to live his vocation. He was no longer able to live this kind of his vocation at Bené-Abbès. He came to Tamanrasset in southern Algeria. This is in the central region of the Sahara with the Ahaggar Mountains (the

---

[6] Charles de Foucauld, Méditations sur les Psaumes, Oeuvres spirituelles (Nouvelle Cité: 1974-1997).

Hoggar) immediately to the west. De Foucauld used the highest point in the region, the Assekrem, as a place of retreat. Living close to the Tuareg, sharing their life of hardships, he made a ten-year study of their language and cultural traditions. He learned the Tuareg language and worked on a dictionary and grammar. His dictionary was published posthumously in four volumes and has become known among Berberologists for its rich descriptions.

Life at Tamanrasset followed the same pattern as Bené-Abbès had. His reputation for kindness and welcome continued and many came to him. A brother, Michel, did come to live with him but did not stay due to the rigours of Charles's life. Charles's catechumen, Paul Embarek, was sent away for a while. This pushed Charles into a deep depression. He did not have the consolation of the Eucharist as he could not say Mass without a server. However he did receive permission to say Mass privately and alone. This helped lift his mood.

For Charles prayer in trust and faith was central to his way of life. Even before his conversion he had a form of faith that sought to know God. "My mind was troubled and searching for the truth, I prayed: My God, if you exist, help me to know you".[7] Later on he said: "God's work is faith: holiness is faith: God's will, perfection, glory, what pleases him supremely in us is faith. Faith in one's heart and in one's deeds together make up true, living faith" (Silent Pilgrimage, p. 22). This is the faith by which he lived.

Faith is what allows us pray with confidence. We see the nothingness of material things. "It puts everything in new light, revealing people as images of God, to be loved and venerated as portraits of our Beloved and to be made recipients of all possible good, and showing us every created thing without exception is then to be used as an aid to getting to Heaven."[8]

The imitation of Christ was central to his way of life. To be one with Christ Jesus was to be in one spirit with him (1 Cor 6:17). He noted in his diary for July 22, 1905:

---

[7] as quoted in René Voillaume, Silent Pilgrimage to God: The Spirituality of Charles de Foucauld (New York: 1977), p. 17.

[8] Charles de Foucauld, writings selected and edited by Robert Ellsberg (Maryknoll: 1999), p. 100.

> Love, obey, imitate – a life of faith, hope, and charity. Love Jesus, obey and imitate him. Obedience will put you into the situation that he wills for you. When his will does not show you clearly that he is willing an alteration in your situation, remain in the status quo. But always imitate him. Without imitation of him, there can be no perfection. In your own case especially, for imitating him is your vocation, duty and obligation at every moment of your life. Imitation of him has always been your first resolution in all your retreats: in capite libri (Heb. 10:7). It stands at the head of your life and gives it its direction. Jesus has put you into the life of Nazareth to stay there forever.[9]

He wanted the order he was trying to found to be a life that imitated Jesus. "One thing only," he said, "should put us to shame: not loving him enough" (Ellsberg, p. 50). Jesus was crowned with thorns so we should not expect a crown of roses. He saw his work as offering himself in sacrifice with Jesus "as a victim for the sanctification of humans" (Spiritual Autobiography, p. 94). Increasingly he saw that he couldn't make converts but he saw the goodness of all people as images of God. He was sure that those who didn't believe would be saved – this wasn't a popular position in Charles' time.

Charles saw the importance of the hidden life of Jesus in Nazareth. For Charles this meant a hidden life living and working among poor people. He saw Jesus as his brother. Charles would imagine himself as a new member of the Holy Family in its life at Nazareth (Silent Pilgrimage, p. 56f). The invisible part of Jesus' life in Nazareth was his inner life. "Your life" he says, "was one continual outpouring into God, a continued gazing at God, enacting contemplation of God at every moment of your life" (Ellsberg, p. 49ff). This was a part of Jesus's life as well as the virtues of poverty and self-effacement.

On May 17, 1906, Charles wrote down 14 resolutions that he adopted while making a retreat between Holy Thursday and Easter Tuesday. They summarise his renewed commitment to living the life of Nazareth in the midst of the desert at Tamanrasset. He begins,

---

[9] Spiritual Autobiography of Charles de Foucauld, edited and commented on by J-F Six (New York: 1964), p. 166.

"1. I must remember to what kind of a life I have been called: the imitation of Jesus of Nazareth; the adoration of the Sacred Host exposed; the silent sanctification of unbelieving peoples by carrying Jesus among them, adoring him and imitating his hidden life." The list continues with resolutions related to Jesus's hidden life: penance; poverty; lowliness; silence; detachment; adoration and interior prayer; zeal for souls; good example, and the like. It closes with, "14. I must remember to let the Heart of Jesus live in my heart, so that it may be no longer I who live, but the Heart of Jesus living in me, as it lived in Nazareth" (Gal. 2:20).

(Spiritual Autobiography, 170-171)

The scriptural text that moved charles was the example of Jesus's hidden life in Nazareth. "And he went down with them and came to Nazareth and was subject to them" (Luke 2:51). Jesus lived a life of labour and obscurity. He was subject to Mary and Joseph. "You were obedient in every way that a good son is obedient" (Spiritual Autobiography, p. 84). In this way he wanted to know love and become love. This was the basis of Charles's imitation of the Hidden Life – to love and welcome all who came to him. "We share" he said "in the peace and happiness of the Divine Beloved depending on how much we are in love" (Silent Pilgrimage, p. 75). Jesus loved all people – especially the poor and outcasts. Charles was devoted to the Holy Eucharist and he spent a large part of each day in adoration of the Blessed Sacrament. "The Holy Eucharist is Jesus, all Jesus… In the Holy Eucharist you are there, my beloved Jesus…" (Silent Pilgrimage, p. 33). He sensed the presence of Jesus all around him. He felt a union with Jesus which he radiated to all. Many people, believers and non-believers alike, loved to be in his presence. They felt loved, accepted and affirmed. He brought comfort and healing to those who came to him.

The End:
The fateful year of 1914 saw Europe plunged into war. Most of the French troops from the Sahara were sent back to France. The Turkish sultan, an ally of Germany, declared a jihad in 1914 against the French, Italians and British. The Italians withdrew from Tripoli which left this area open to the Senussi Brotherhood, a fundamentalist Muslim group founded in 1840 to oppose European Colonialism. In March of 1916 the Senussi moved on the

French in Algeria and took Fort Djanet which was only 310 miles from Tamanrasset. Since June 1915 Brother Charles laboured to convert the hermitage into a kind of fort where he could protect the people who came to him. As at Béne-Abbès, many made their way to Charles. He was known for his kindness and healings. There was a small community of Haratins and Tuareg at Tamanrasset. In mid 1916 The French commanders left in the Sahara urged Charles to go to fort Motylinski. Charles refused to leave those who had come to depend on him.

A plot was hatched among the Senussi to kidnap Charles. A man known to Charles, El Modani, agreed to betray him. He called at the fort. Charles opened the door. Charles was kidnapped and two soliders arrived. In the ensuing melee Charles was shot and died. Mohammed had told his followers to respect the "people of the Book" and to respect the Holy men of other faiths. The killing of Charles was a great shock to many Muslims. Charles had written: "Unless the grain of wheat dies, it remains alone: but if it dies, it brings forth much fruit (see John 12:29ff). I have not died, so I am alone. Pray for my conversion, that dying, I may bear fruit" (Ellsberg, 90).

To the eyes of the world we live in Charles's death seemed a disaster. He had no followers. He died anonymously in the desert like so many victims of war. In many of the wars fought today there are so many anonymous people and especially children who die. They are just statistics to many. When we can put a face on one of the victims like Charles, they become real.

John Donne, in his poem "No Man is an Island", wrote:

> "No man is an island,
> Entire of itself,
> Every man is a piece of the continent,
> A part of the main.
> If a clod be washed away by the sea,
> Europe is the less.
> As well as if a promontory were.
> As well as if a manor of thy friend's
> Or of thine own were:
> Any man's death diminishes me,

Because I am involved in mankind,
And therefore never send to know for whom the bell tolls;
It tolls for thee."

We are a very diminished people because of the death and agony of so many. We are all part of humankind – yet so many innocent die.

Yet for Charles this was not the end. His prayer was like a rich underground river giving life to the church. In the order of the world he was a failure, yet the Holy Spirit breathed in him. He had helped organise a confraternity in France in support of his ideas. This organisation, the "Association of the Brothers and Sisters of the Sacred Heart of Jesus", consisted of 48 lay and ordained at the time of his death. Louis Massignon was a member of this group. Another was René Bazin who wrote a biography of Charles "La Vie de Charles de Foucauld: Explorateur en Maroc, ermite du Sahara" (1923). Charles's fame began to spread. Groups such as the Little Brothers and the Little Sisters of Jesus were formed. 18 other religious orders and associations were inspired by him. Charles touched the hearts of many and led them to God. René Voillaume (+2003) and Sister Magdalene of Jesus (+1989) were among his followers and founders of orders. In 1936 a film called "The Call of Silence" came out depicting the life of Charles. Charles was beatified on 13 November 2005 by Cardinal José Saraiva Martins and canonised on 15 May 2022 in St. Peter's Square, by Pope Francis. His feast day is 1 December. He is also honoured by the Church of England and the Episcopal Church on the same day. He is highly respected in the Muslim world. He had served the poorest of the poor of the Islamic world. Charles wrote:[10]

> "Jesus came to Nazareth, the place of a hidden life, of ordinary life, of family life, of prayer, work, obscurity, silent virtues, practices with no witnesses other than God, his friends and neighbours. Nazareth is the place where most people direct their lives. We must infinitely respect the least of our brothers [and sisters]. Let us mingle with them. Let us be one of them to the extent that God wishes and let us treat them fraternally in order to have the honour and joy of being accepted as one of them."

---

[10] Robert Ellsberg, 'Charles de Foucauld', in Martyrs, ed. Susan Bergmann (Maryknoll: 1998), p. 297.

Chapter 6

Prayer of Abandonment: Charles and Thérèse

St. Paul wrote in Romans 8: "And we know that for those who love God all things work together for good, for those who are called according to his purpose." (Romans 8:28). In the lives of Charles and Thérèse they lived out in radical faith trust that in all the trials of their lives. This was the basis of their abandonment (abandon in French) to the will of God. Charles showed this in several instances of his life. On August 11, 1906, right outside the hermitage of Tamanrasset, Charles was bitten on the foot by a horned viper, a desert snake whose venom is nearly always fatal. Charles lost consciousness. His friend captain Motylinski called Mohamed ben Hamida, the native soldier who was his guide. The man employed drastic measures: red hot iron on the wound and three bleedings to keep the poison from invading the body. Charles survived but was not well. Then a great thing happened. The nomads, who had seemed indifferent, mobilised. They saw that the Christian Marabout had loved them. They surrounded him and even though they were poor they sold a lot of what they had to get special foods and milk to build him up. They were brothers and sisters to him. He was their brother and they, in turn, were brothers and sisters to him. Good had come from his near-death experience.

Charles's prayer of Abandonment reads as follows:

> 'Father, I abandon myself into your hands, do with me what you will.
> Whatever you may do, I thank you: I am ready for all, I accept all.
> Let only your will be done in me and in all your creatures.
> I wish no more than this, O Lord. Into your hands, I commend my soul;
> I offer it to you with all the love of my heart;
> For I love you, Lord, and so need to give myself:

> To surrender myself into your hands without reserve and with boundless confidence. For you are my Father.'

As a loving Father God is worthy of our complete trust. Such an act of faith comes from someone who has come to trust that what God wants is best for us and our brothers and sisters, despite how difficult it seems to us at the time. Thérèse in her time had seen God as a loving and caring Father and she trusted in his love and mercy. She did not see weakness as an obstacle in her life but she saw this as an opportunity to rely on God's grace and grow in abandonment and trust. "For when I am weak then I am strong" (2 Cor 12:10), St. Paul tells us. Her giving herself to trust and abandonment to God was the secret of Thérèse's Little Way: "Unless you become like a little child you shall not enter the kingdom of God" (Matt 18:3).

St. Thérèse said:

> "I understand so well that it is only love which makes us acceptable to God – that this love is the only good I ambition. Jesus deigned to show me the road that leads to this Divine Furnace, and this road is the surrender of the little child who sleeps without fear in its Father's arms.
> I had a certainty of going far away from this land of sadness and gloom one day – it had been given to me as early as my childhood… I felt the desire for a more beautiful place from the bottom of my heart… another place will provide me a stable home. But, all of a sudden, the fog which surrounds me becomes even thicker; it penetrates my soul and surrounds me in such a way that I cannot find the gentle image of my homeland there anymore, and everything disappears."
> (St. Thérèse and the Healing of Abandonment [Society of the Little Flower: Arpil 8, 2020])

Jesus and all his brothers and sisters are starved of love.

Thérèse wrote:

> "Jesus does not demand great actions from us but simply surrender and gratitude. Has he not said … 'OFFER TO GOD THE SACRIFICES OF PRAISE AND THANKSGIVING'

(cf. Psalm 49:14). see, then, all that Jesus lays claim to from us; He has no need of our works but only of our love ... I feel it more than ever before, Jesus is parched, for He meets only the ungrateful and indifferent among His disciples in the world, and among His own disciples, alas, He finds few hearts who surrender to Him without reservations, who understand the real tenderness of His infinite Love.

(Ms C, IV°)

Thérèse remarks John 4 where Jesus asks the Samaritan woman for a drink. He was in need and she responded. Thérèse lived out her prayer of abandonment when she suffered greatly in the last period of her life. She felt abandoned and she felt the loss of God. She shared in Jesus's suffering servant vocation. Yet through her suffering she reached man and brought healing and light to the broken. Charles was the universal brother! Thérèse was the universal sister!

Thérèse and the Night of Faith:
When Charles was in the Trappist monastery of Akbès he made an offering of himself to Jesus. At the same time Thérèse made an offering of herself to Jesus. On 8 September 1896 she wrote:

(To my dear Sister Marie of the Sacred Heart)
O Jesus, my Beloved, who could express the tenderness and sweetness with which You are guiding my soul! It pleases You to cause the rays of Your grace to shine through even in the midst of the darkest storm! Jesus, the storm was raging very strongly in my soul ever since the beautiful feast of Your victory, the radiant feast of Easter; one Saturday in the month of May, thinking of the mysterious dreams which are granted at times to certain souls, I said to myself that these dreams must be a very sweet consolation, and yet I wasn't asking for such a consolation.

(Ms B, 5)

Her vocation was to be 'love in the heart of the Church' (Ms B, 3V°). The Holy Spirit is love in the heart of the Church. Thérèse was led by the Holy Spirit to embody this love in her person. At the same time Charles wrote:

"My God, I give my soul into your hands: I give this, with all the love of my heart, because I love you and it is a need for me to give myself, to place everything in your hands without measure." He modeled himself on Jesus's total giving of himself to the Father. "Into your hands I commit my spirit" (Luke 23:46). In contemplating Jesus on the cross we see that God is Father with a maternal heart. The child knows that it depends on the love of Father and Mother. This is the love of Jesus trusting in God even in his agony. Thérèse and Charles follow him in this. St. Paul reminds us "… in all these things we are more than conquerors through him who love us" (Rom 8:37). Jesus, in his resurrection, carried the wounds of his suffering and he gave us the gift of the Spirit.

Leonard Cohen wrote a novel in 1966 called 'Beautiful Losers'. It revolves around four central and flawed characters. It has a nameless narrator, his wife Edith, their domineering friend and mentor F and Catherine Tekakwitha, a 17th century Mohawk saint. He explores friendship, sex and spirituality. Cohen wrote the book while he was living on the Greek island of Hydra in 1964 and 1965. He fasted and consumed amphetamines to focus his creativity.

In one of the chapters he looks at the lives of the ones we call saints.

> "A saint is someone who has achieved a remote human possibility. It is impossible to say what that possibility is. I think it has something to do with the energy of love. Contact with this energy results in the exercise of a kind of balance in the chaos of existence. A saint does not dissolve the chaos; if he did the world would have changed long ago. I do not think that a saint dissolves the chaos even for himself, for there is something arrogant and warlike in the notion of a man setting the universe in order. It is a kind of balance that is his glory. He rides the drifts like an escaped ski. His course is a caress of the hill."[1]

Existence is chaotic but the saint shows us an alternative way of being in the world. Charles and Thérèse were like this. Over the years many have come to know them and their love reaches beyond the grave. The Holy

---

[1] Leonard Cohen, Beautiful Losers (London: 2009 edition), p. 99.

Spirit continues his work in them and through them. During the First World War many French soldiers felt lost and abandoned. They were sacrificed by higher powers. Their morale was low. Thérèse's autobiography 'The Story of a Soul' became very popular with the troops. They felt the comfort of her love and it sustained them in dark days. She felt alone at the end of her life "at the table of sinners". She was one with those who felt this loneliness.

Cohen goes on to say:

> "Something in him so loves the world that he gives himself to the laws of gravity and chance. Far from flying with the angels, he traces with the fidelity of a seismograph needle the state of the solid bloody landscape. His house is dangerous and finite, but he is at home in the world. He can love the shapes of human beings, the fine and twisted shapes of the heart. It is good to have among us such men, such balancing monsters of love. It makes me think that the numbers in the bag actually correspond to the numbers on the raffles we have bought so dearly, and so the prize is not an illusion."
>
> (Beautiful Losers, p. 9)

It is good to have such people among us. The evil, the betrayals, the violence of our world can feel overwhelming. The saints do not fly above this as some disinterested spirit. They are flesh and blood and live in the midst of all this pain. They know the "fine and twisted shapes" of the human heart. The can love "the shapes of human beings". Charles and Thérèse brought this love to bear in our world. They are a counter-sign to so much of what we see.

Thérèse's long suffering and loneliness began on the 5th April, 1896 on Easter day. She saw the appearance of hemoptysis due to Tuberculosis. She was given a special share in Jesus's sufferings. She suffered mentally, physically and spiritually. She was in agony. She was amazed at those who had no faith. She was was amazed that they could go on and not commit suicide (Ms C, 5V°). Thérèse experienced a night of no hope in which she could no longer think of Heaven. She expresses her pain and loneliness in the following passage:

"I was saying that the certainty of going away one day far from the sad and dark country had been given me from the day of my childhood. I did not believe this only because I heard it from persons much more knowledgeable than I, but I felt in the bottom of my heart real longings for this most beautiful country. Just as the genius of Christopher Columbus gave him a presentiment of a new world when nobody had even thought of such a thing; so also I felt that another land would one day serve me as a permanent dwelling place. Then suddenly the fog that surrounds me becomes more dense; it penetrates my soul and envelops it in such a way that it is impossible to discover within it the sweet image of my Fatherland; everything has disappeared! When I want to rest my heart fatigued by the darkness that surrounds it by the memory of the luminous country after which I aspire, my torment redoubles; it seems to me that the darkness, borrowing the voices of sinners, says mockingly to me: "You are dreaming about the light, about a fatherland embalmed in the sweetest perfumes; you are dreaming about the eternal possession of the Creator of all these marvels; you believe that one day you will walk out of this fog that surrounds you! Advance, advance; rejoice in death which will give you not what you hope for but a night still more profound, the night of nothingness."

Dear Mother, the image I wanted to give you of the darkness that obscures my soul is as imperfect as a sketch is to the model; however, I don't want to write any longer about it; I fear I might blaspheme; I fear even that I have already said too much.

(MsC 6v°-7r°)

The 'night of nothingness' is the great fear of us all. Does any effort matter? There are so many of us, are we of any importance? What if at the end of the day there was nothing? Thérèse felt this great temptation against faith.

Charles felt this pain as well. He was worried when he made so few converts. One man called Br. Michel did come to him. He stayed for a while. He was very impressed with Charles. Br. Michel (real name Jean-Marie Goyat) had been a novice with the White Fathers. He had an ardent faith but could be unstable. He would say of Charles: "He loved Jesus Christ passionately and his great happiness was in communing with the sacrament of love, really present in the tabernacle."[2] Michel saw him give away all he had to the poor. In 1906 his reputation was such that there was always a great celebration when Charles entered a village. However Michel's health couldn't put up with the rigors of Charles's life. The adventure was over for Michel and in 1907 he abandoned his project. Charles was without a follower. He had to face his own disappointment. He had felt a darkness in Akbès when he could not see a way forward. This was when he wrote his prayer of abandonment. He had to battle with this darkness and leave all in the hands of God.

Thérèse knew the pain of so many people who felt they had no hope. In meditating on the face of the Crucified One she saw the faces of so many who suffered – often in silence and alone. She shared in Jesus's suffering. He was absent and hidden. In the faces of those who suffer she saw Jesus. The prophet Isaiah said: "In all our afflictions he was afflicted" (Isa 63:9). Our distress is his. Thérèse felt a communion with those who feel they cannot believe. She saw them too as her sisters and brothers and she loved them. Thérèse continued to love God in this 'night of nothingness' and this helps us understand the prayer of abandonment. She trusted that Jesus loved us. She remembered his agony in Gethsemane, the same night as he instituted the Eucharist. Charles, independently of Thérèse, saw it was through the cross that Jesus triumphed. He left us a memorial in the Eucharist and Charles would spend hours in adoration. He surrendered all into the hands of God. Charles read Jesus's words: "Father, why have you abandoned me?" In response Charles said: "Father, I abandon myself to you." This showed his love. Just before his martyrdom he wrote to Marie de Bondy. He had the option of leaving Tamanrasset and going to a safe place but he refused. He would stay with the poor ones who depended on him. He said to her: "How true it is, we shall never love enough" (Antier, p. 437). Within a month of writing this he was martyred. "No greater love has a man than this, that he lay down his life for his friends" (Jn 15:13). He wrote to Marie de Bondy in an earlier time that he would turn nobody away who knocked on his door (Antier, p. 349). This cost him his life.

---

[2] Jean-Jacques Antier, Charles de Foucauld (San Francisco: 2022), p. 342.

Father:
Charles did not remember much of his father. Thérèse had happy memories of her childhood. Charles was fond of praying the 'Our Father' (see Mt 6:9). He felt he was held by the love of God. Colonel de Morlet took the place of Charles's earthly father. Charles in his early prayers used the term 'My God'. As he grew in intimacy with Jesus he would say 'Father'. He saw that "this is love: not that we loved God, but that he loved us and sent his son as an atoning sacrifice for our sins" (1 Jn 4:10). To pray is to listen to God the Father speaking to us by the Holy Spirit. Charles said we allow God to direct our lives. He doesn't allow despair to overcome us. God's peace invades our hearts even in the midst of great tribulation. As St. Paul said, "The Spirit you received does not make you slaves, so that you live in fear again; rather, the Spirit you received brought about your adoption to sonship. And by him we cry, "Abba, Father." " (Rom 8:15). In the Book of Isaiah we read...

> But Zion said: "The Lord has forsaken me"
> ...
> Can a mother forget the baby at her breast
>   and have no compassion on the child she has borne?
>   Though she may forget,
>   I will not forget you!
> See, I have engraved you on the palms of my hands;
>   your walls are ever before me.
>   (Isa 49:14-16)

God is greater than our terms Father or Mother. He is the source of all love and we are the ones he loves. He loves us like a mother and even more than any mother. Through the eyes of Thérèse and Charles we are pointed to that love and live in that love. They call us to abandon ourselves into the arms of this Father. They believed in the love of God revealed in Jesus and that nothing could separate us from that love.

> No, in all these things we are more than conquerors through him who loved us. For I am convinced that neither death nor life, neither angels nor demons, neither the present nor the future, nor any powers, neither height nor depth, nor anything else in all creation, will be able to separate us from the love of God that is in Christ Jesus our Lord.
>   (Rom 8:37-40)

John tells us "God is love" (1 Jn 4:8, 16). This is the love Thérèse and Charles experienced and they felt called to live that love in the Spirit and share it with others.

We are a need of God. He reaches out in love and he hopes we will respond. Love for love! Charles saw that 'abandonment (abandon)' did not mean doing nothing. We have to learn to respond in love. Jesus on the cross is the model for 'abandon'. "Father, into your hands I commend my spirit." (Luke 23:46). Mary, his mother, is a model as well. She did not fully understand what God wanted of her when he announced she would become the mother of Jesus. Her response, nonetheless, was: "Be it done unto me according to thy word" (Lk 1:38). She left all in the hands of God. She assented to God's will even though she did not fully understand.

The idea of 'abandon' (abandonment) was something that was found in French Spirituality. Jean Pierre de Caussade (+1751) wrote 'Abandonment to Divine Providence'. He was spiritual director to the Visitation nuns at Nancy and he wrote it for them. He was influenced by Francis de Sales and John of the Cross.

Father Jerome, the abbot of Notre-Dame des Neiges knew this book. Thérèse also knew of this work. Her aunt, Sister Dosithée, had been a Visitation nun. Her mother Zélie read this book when she developed cancer. The abandonment calls one to serenity and confidence in God's work in us even when all seems bleak. God is present with us in every moment of our lives. Abandon means we acknowledge his presence and live in his love, even if he appears to be absent. We live each moment under the guidance of the Holy Spirit. Abandonment is another way of saying we love you.

Charles spoke of not knowing the plan of God but of giving oneself totally in trust to him. God reveals himself in the details of our lives. By remaining open to God's revelation to us in the moments of our lives, both small and great, we grow in love. Every moment reveals God to us if we become alive to his presence among us. He is with us always – we are not always with him. Francis de Sales in his work "Treatise on the Love of God (Traité de l'Amour de Dieu)" says that by submitting to the will of God we show true love. By doing this our love grows. We show great confidence when we practice this abandonment. De Caussade refers to self-abandonment and simplicity in the manner of Francis de Sales. He also spoke of how the Holy

Spirit cleanses and enlightens the soul – after John of the Cross. He speaks of 'abandonment (abandon)', trust, confidence and surrender in his work. Charles's prayer was the prayer of Jesus, "… Not as I will, but as you will" (Matt 26:39). Edith Stein and Dietrich Bonhoeffer knew the horrors of the concentration camps. Yet they never ceased to pray for liberation and for those suffering with them.

A Broken Hallelujah (הָיְ וּלְלָה (hallū yāh))

People sometimes feel looking at Charles and Thérèse that they are inadequate. However Leonard Cohen shows us in his work "Hallelujah" that the broken and confused belong and there is forgiveness and acceptance in God's hands. The song says:

> Now I've heard there was a secret chord
> That David played, and it pleased the Lord
> But you don't really care for music, do you?
> It goes like this, the fourth, the fifth
> The minor falls, the major lifts
> The baffled king composing hallelujah
> Hallelujah, Hallelujah
> Hallelujah, Hallelujah
>
> Your faith was strong but you needed proof
> You saw her bathing on the roof
> Her beauty and the moonlight overthrew you
> She tied you to a kitchen chair
> She broke your throne, and she cut your hair
> And from your lips she drew the hallelujah
> Hallelujah, Hallelujah
> Hallelujah, Hallelujah
>
> Baby I've been here before
> I've seen this room and I've walked this floor
> I used to live alone before I knew you
> I've seen your flag on the marble arch
> But love is not a victory march
> It's a cold and it's a broken hallelujah
> Hallelujah, Hallelujah
> Hallelujah, Hallelujah

> Well there was a time when you let me know
> What's really going on below
> But now you never show that to me do you
> But remember when I moved in you
> And the holy ghost was moving too
> And every breath we drew was hallelujah
> Hallelujah, Hallelujah
> Hallelujah, Hallelujah
>
> Well, maybe there's a God above
> But all I've ever learned from love
> Was how to shoot somebody who outdrew you
> It's not a cry that you hear at night
> It's not somebody who's seen the light
> It's a cold and it's a broken hallelujah
> Hallelujah, Hallelujah
> Hallelujah, Hallelujah

The poem-song begins with David playing the secret chord. There is a tradition in Judaism (in the Talmud)[3] that David work up at night to play the secret chord that pleased the Lord. Cohen belongs to that line of singers who play for the Lord. Even though David's faith was strong he entered into an adulterous relationship with Bathsheba. She becomes pregnant and David arranges for the death of her husband, Uriah the Hittite. In 2 Samuel 12 the prophet Nathan confronts David. David is forgiven but his sin leads to destruction and ill-fortune for him and his family. Cohen says:

> "Her beauty and the moonlight overthrew you
> She tied you to her kitchen chair
> She broke your throne and she cut your hair
> And from your lips she drew the hallelujah."

David's son Solomon, at once wise and foolish, set in train the breaking up of the kingdom… "She broke your throne". David's son, Absalom, rebelled against him. In 2 Samuel 14:25 he was described as the handsomest man in the kingdom. He named himself king. Absalom caught his hair in branches and was killed by David's soldiers. David's grief was violent. He cried out:

---

[3] see Harry Freedman, Leonard Cohen: The Mystical Roots of Genius (London: 2021), p. 61-73.

> "O my son Absalom, my son Absalom!
> Would God I had died for thee, O Absalom, my son, my son!"
>
> (2 Sam 18:33)

David withdrew to the city of Mahanaim in mourning until Joab roused him "from the extravagance of his grief" and called him to fulfill his duty to his people. (2 Sam 19:1-8). Cohen tells this story in the words "she cut your hair". Yet through all this David sings his hallelujah, but now a broken one. It is now a cold and broken Hallelujah. We are often broken like David but he still praises God in his grief and allows God work through him.

The song-poem references people like Saul, David Samson, Absalom and David's children. They all live in a confused and broken world. They fail but still they turn to God. This hallelujah is not a sentimental one, singing praise of God. It is a "broken and cold" hallelujah because they come to accept their brokenness and still praise God – Hallelujah.

> "There is a crack in everything
> That's how the light gets in."
>
> (Anthem: 1992)

This is another form of self-surrender. God is greater than our failings. By accepting his forgiveness, like Charles did, we can allow his light to come in and we can begin anew.

Cohen says "I didn't even know the name". The one who didn't know God's name was Moses – the name that should not be taken in vain. As a young man, at the Burning Bush, Moses came to know the Name (Ex 3) but in his old age he took it in vain (Num 20:8-11). According to the Zohar, God's name was written on his staff. The Name mattered to Cohen. He wrote G-d instead of God. This came from his Jewish tradition. Words mean a lot. The world came into existence through words. In the first chapter of Genesis God created the world through speech: "And God said, let there be light, And there was light" (Gen 1:3). In the Gospel of John we read: "In the beginning was the Word and the Word was with God and the Word was God" (Jn 1:1). Names are important because they encapsulate our essence. Cohen didn't approve of people changing their names. He was thinking of those who had come to Canada and the US from Eastern Europe. In his "Book of Mercy" he said: "I always feel that the world was created through words through words, through speech in our tradition and I've always seen the enormous light in charged speech, and that's what I've tried to get to."[4] There's a blaze of light in every word.

Our words, our writings and what they say have an influence on others. Words used in hate generate hate. Words misused against groups lead to hatred of that group. Racism, bigotry come from these words. Words that come from God lead us to seek God and his ways. They seek to lead us to love but it is a lifelong journey to understand God's word. When we try to live God's word we change. Charles and Thérèse meditated often on the word of God and they had fascinating insights. We don't always understand and that is why Cohen speaks of a "Broken Hallelujah".

> "I did my best, it wasn't much,
> I couldn't feel, so I tried to touch"
> There was nothing on his tongue but Hallelujah.

Cohen spoke about Hallelujah when he played in Warsaw in 1985: "I know that there is an eye that watches all of us. There is a judgement that weighs everything we do. And before this great force, which is greater than any government, I stand in awe and I kneel in respect. And it is to this great judgement that I dedicate this next song: 'Hallelujah'." (Freedman, Leonard Cohen, p 75). Even if we feel lost and broken we can still sing alleluia and let the light in. This is the world created by the words of Hallelujah.

---

[4] CBS Radio Interview with Robert Sward, 1984: reproduced in Burger, Leonard Cohen on Leonard Cohen.

Chapter 7

Dance Me to the End of Love

Leonard Cohen (+2016) was a Canadian singer-songwriter, poet and novelist. Themes he commonly explored were faith and morality, isolation and depression, social and political conflict, and love, desire, regret and loss. He began his career as a poet and novelist in the 1950s and early 1960s. His music career did not begin until 1967. He was disappointed with his lack of success as an author and he entered the folk circuit as a singer-songwriter. He was familiar with Andy Warhol's "Factory" crowd. Judy Collins recorded his song "Suzanne" and this was a hit for her. Cohen did not have any faith in his guitar playing and singing, but Collins did and she pushed him to go on stage.

> And then he played me "Suzanne" ... I said, "Leonard, you must come with me to this big fundraiser I'm doing" ... Jimi Hendrix was on it. He'd never sung [in front of a large audience] before then. He got out on stage and started singing. Everybody was going crazy—they loved it. And he stopped about halfway through and walked off the stage. Everybody went nuts. ... They demanded that he come back. And I demanded; I said, "I'll go out with you." So we went out, and we sang it. And of course, that was the beginning.
> (December 4, 2017, at the Wayback Machine, The Globe and Mail, Canada, November 11, 2016)

She began to introduce him in her concerts. He came to the attention of Columbia Records producer, John Hammond, who signed Cohen to a record deal. His first album was "Songs of Leonard Cohen". In his music and poetry Cohen shows the whole act of living contains immense amounts of sorrow and hopelessness and despair. The act of living also involves passion, high hopes, deep love and eternal love.

In late 2005 Cohen's daughter, Lorca, was told there was trouble with Cohen's money. They discovered most of the money in his account was gone. He had to go back on the road to recoup some of his losses.

He published a book of poetry and drawings in May 2006. Between 2008 and 2010 he went on a world tour. He'd died in 2016. The New York Times wrote about him after his death:

> "Epic and Enigmatic Songwriter"
> Over a musical career that spanned nearly five decades, Mr. Cohen wrote songs that addressed—in spare language that could be both oblique and telling—themes of love and faith, despair and exaltation, solitude and connection, war and politics.[143]
> It's inevitable that Mr. Cohen will be remembered above all for his lyrics. They are terse and acrobatic, scriptural and bawdy, vividly descriptive and enduringly ambiguous, never far from either a riddle or a punch line.
> (The New York Times: Obituary, Nov. 10, 2016, and "An Appraisa", Nov. 11, 2016)

Cohen's Influences:

Listening to Cohen and reading his poetry we detect a spiritual influence.[1] Cohen wrote a song "I Can't Forget" which he recorded on the "I'm Your Man" album (1988). He imagined it would be a song about the exodus of the Hebrew children from Egypt, which was intended as a metaphor for the freeing of the soul from bondage. He recalled:

> "When I went in to record the vocal for the track, however, I found I couldn't get the words out of my throat. I couldn't sing the words because I wasn't entitled to speak of the emancipation of the spirit."[2]

---

[1] see Harry Freedman, Leonard Cohen: The Mystical Roots of Genius (London: 2021), p. 31.
[2] Interview with Kristine McKenna, LA Weekly, March 1988.

He questioned himself and his faith. It was a journey he was on. The Bible was always a part of this life. This included the New Testament and he thought much about the Book of Revelation. He spoke of the Book of Revelation to his friends when he lived in Hydra. He said later in life:

> "So, the Book of Revelation is a kind of manual. It's wonderful poetry and it's wonderful revelation and it certainly does fulfill that great characteristic of charged writing by pulling the rug out from under you, and you are in a new world, and there is a new Jerusalem, and you are ready to embrace the notion of newness and rebirth and of a new cosmos, and it invites you to unfold that reality in your own heart and in your own life, that dissolving of time."
> (Interview with Leonard Cohen, CBC, August 1995)

He said you could see the figure of Jesus in the pages of the New Testament. When his son Adam was in a coma after a car crash Cohen sat by his bed and read from the prophet Isaiah to him. When Adam came to he asked: "Dad, can you read something else?"[3]

In his songs he doesn't stay with the literal text but re-interprets it for today. In his song "Story of Isaac" (1969) he turned Isaac's story into a protest against the way people are willing to sacrifice others for absurd ideals. "Born in Chains" is a song that becomes a sanctification of human love. He also knew the Talmud and the Zohar. The Talmud is the central text of Rabbinic Judaism and is the primary source of Jewish religious law and Jewish theology. The Zohar is a mystical work of the Kabbalah. In his 1992 song "Anthem" Cohen borrows a phrase from the Kabbalah. The song includes the words: "There is a crack in everything, that's how the light gets in". He quoted these in a new way to offer perspectives on our soul and God.

---

[3] quoted in Sylvie Simmons, I'm Your Man: The Life of Leonard Cohen (London: 2013), p. 350.

The Holocaust also had an influence on him. His song "Dance Me to the End of Love" (1988) has a line about burning violins. This came about when he saw a photograph of inmates in a concentration camp being forced to play violins.

Rashi (+1105) was a Jewish biblical commentator par excellence. He is referred to as Rashi, an acronym of his full name Rabbi Shlomo Yitzchaki. He live in Troyes, on the river Seine. His style is accessible and easy to understand. He could communicate with just a few words where it would take others many words. Cohen would have studied the Bible with Rashi's commentary at Herzliah High School. This would have prepared Cohen for his later study of the Talmud.

At a young age Cohen had an Irish nanny. She would bring him to Mass on a Sunday. Cohen did not convert but all of these influences spread into his songs and poetry. Cohen did not see Christianity and Judaism as being at odds but rather thought they could work together. Cohen experienced many difficulties in life – disappointments, broken relationships, addictions and depression. His writing helped him cope with these things. Jonathan Sacks (+2020), an orthodox rabbi who served as chief Rabbi of the United Hebrew Congregation of the Commonwealth, said of Cohen: Leonard Cohen taught us that even in the midst of darkness there is light; in the midst of hatred there is love, with our dying breath we can still sing Hallelujah.

One of the spiritual disciplines that had a great effect on his life was the Rinzai form of Buddhism which he learned from the Japanese Zen master, Joshu Sasaki Roshi. Cohen spent long periods with Roshi at his monastery in Mount Baldy, in California. He moved there permanently in 1996 and after three years he became a Buddisht monk. Roshi, his teacher, was the main reason he studied Zen. He said of Roshi: "I liked what he said, and I liked who he was and I began to study with him ... And I suppose if he had been a professor of Physics in Heidelberg, I should have learned German and studied physics, but he happened to be an old monk, so I began to study with him on his own terms.[4]

---

[4] Interview with Alberto Manzano, El Europeo, Spring 1993.

He doesn't reference Zen in his music or poetry. It was a spiritual discipline for him where he deepened his thought and faith. He never saw a conflict between Buddhism and Judaism or Christianity explaining: "there is no prayerful worship and there is no discussion of a deity."[5] In 1994 Cohen felt like he was losing his sanity after a tour. This is when he turned to Buddhism. His battle with mental health was a struggle that forced him to spend his life looking for coping mechanisms. It made him drink to excess, or womanise to excess just to get away from the torture of his depressive thoughts. After touring for his album, The Future, he was drinking four bottles of wine a day. He sought help in the Mount Baldy Zen Buddhist monastery in California. There he came under the influence of Roshi who "seemed to be at ease with himself and at ease with others". However he never really found the peace he was looking for and left the community in 1999. However his experience reinforced his relationship with his faith and taught him that one didn't need a lot of luxuries to survive. His search and longing continued, but he had learned a lot.

He battled with depression all his life. When he was young he enrolled at Columbia, studying English and writing stories. He wrote a manical short novel, 'Ballet of Lepers'. It was reworked and published in 2022 in a posthumous collection of fiction by Cohen. He began to write poetry and he discovered Federico del Sagrado de Jesus Garcia Lorca (1898-1936), known as Federico Garcia Lorca. He was a Spanish poet, playwright and theatre director. He belonged to a group called the Generation of '27, a group consisting mostly of poets who introduced such European movements as Symbolism, Futurism and Surrealism into Spanish literature.

He initially rose to fame with 'Romancero Gitano' (Gypsy Ballads) a book of poems about his native Andalusia. His poetry incorporated Andalusian motifs and avant-garde styles. He went to New York from 1929 to 1930. This was documented posthumously in 'Poeta en Nueva York' (Poet in New York, 1942). He returned to Spain and wrote his best-known plays – 'Blood Wedding' (1932), 'Yerma' (1934), and 'The House of Bernarda Alba' (1936).

---

[5] "I am the little Jew who wrote the Bible" – A conversation between Leonard Cohen and Arthur Kurzwell, quoted in Freedman, Leonard Cohen, p. 13.

Garcia Lorca was gay and suffered much from depression. He suffered in his relationships. Garcia Lorca was killed by the Nationalist forces at the outbreak of the Spanish Civil War. He had been friendly with Salvador Dali and filmmaker Luis Buñuel. Lorca's poetry portrays in words the same surrealistic view of the world.

Cohen first came across Lorca in 1950, while he was still a teenager. He was browsing in a second hand bookshop when he picked up Lorca's 'Selected Poems'. He discovered the poem 'Gacela of the Morning Market'. On stage, Cohen would often recite the opening lines:

> "Through the Arch of Elvira,
> I want to see you go,
> So that I can learn your name,
> And break into tears."

"Lorca" said Cohen "led me into the racket of poetry. He educated me. He taught me to understand the dignity of sorrow through flamenco music and to be deeply touched by the dancing image of a Gypsy man and woman. Thanks to him, Spain entered my mind at 15, and later I became influenced by the civil war folk song music."[6] Lorca's style freed Cohen to explore the effect of language and how to use it. Cohen's song "Take this Waltz" is a translate of Lorca's poem "Pequeño Vals Vienés". He called his daughter Lorca in honour of the poet.

He was also fascinated with the Persian poet known as Rumi (Jalal ad-Din Rumi). He understood Rumi's finding of being a stranger in a host culture not wholly one's own. Rumi was born in 1207. He grew up in Tajikistan. Forced to flee their home as a result of the Mongol invasion, his family wandered for many years before settling in Konya, Anatolia, now part of Turkey. Rumi was influenced by a wandering dervish, Shams-of-Tabriz who helped Rumi study the mysteries of the higher world. Shams disappeared mysteriously in 1247. Grief-stricken Rumi found his solace in poetry. He was, according to Leonard Cohen, "in the same league as King David".[7]

---

[6] Leonard Cohen, 18 October 1986 in Toronto Star.
[7] Interview with Elizabeth Boleman-Herring, The Athenian, 1988, quoted in Jeff Burger (ed.), Leonard Cohen on Leonard Cohen (Chicago: 2015).

In the line notes for his 1979 album 'Recent Songs' Cohen wrote that he owed his thanks to his childhood friend Robert Hershon "...who many years ago, put into my hands the books of the old Persian poets Attar and Rumi, whose imagery influenced several songs, especially 'The Guests' and 'The Window'."

Not all of Cohen's influences had a direct impact on his literary style. Some of his most important influences were those who encouraged him in his work. One of the influences was Irving Layton, a Montreal Jew like Cohen, though 20 years older. Once he had been regarded as Canada's outstanding poet. He encouraged Cohen when he began to write and welcomed him into his small select band of young poets of which Layton was the leading light. He and Cohen became close friends. Layton enlightened the process of writing poetry for Cohen. Another who influenced him was Louis Dudek. Dudek taught Leonard Cohen at McGill University and in 1956 his McGill Poetry Series published Cohen's first poetry collection, 'Let Us Compare Mythologies'. Cohen described Dudek as a magnificent teacher.

A third Montreal poet, A. M. Klein, had an impact on Cohen's self perception as a poet. Klein was a leading figure in the Canadian-Jewish literary world. When Cohen met him he was struggling with his mental health. Cohen realised the extent of the sacrifice Klein had made for his art.

In 1963 Leonard Cohen gave a speech in Montreal's Public Library: "I believe that the God worshipped in our synagogues is a hideous distortion of a supreme idea – and deserves to be attacked and destroyed." Cohen blamed Klein's breakdown on the destructive influence of the Jewish community. He felt they were obsessed with business and institutes. They had shamed the old traditions of scholarship and learning. Klein, he said, had acted as a priest to preserve the treasures of old but he was alone. This, Cohen said, led to his isolation and loneliness. "He spoke to men who despised the activity he loved most. He chose to be a priest and protect the dead ritual. And now we have his silence." What was needed was a prophet – one follows ideas as they fluctuate, change, mutate. After this Cohen decided to go into exile. He lived on the island of Hydra for a few years. Love, for Cohen, was sacred, the physical counterpart of the human quest for the divine. He was very fond of the Biblical "Song of Songs", the erotic book of the Old Testament. Both the synagogue and church saw this as a metaphor for God's love for his people and the human person. On Hydra he had moderated success as a poet and writer but he left Hydra to pursue a career in music – at the time just writing music.

Cohen wrote "Suzanne" and "Dress Rehearsal Rag" which he sent to Judy Collins. She recorded them on her album "In My Life". The album was a success and people began to talk about Leonard Cohen. He thought there could be a new religion. This was about 1967 when people thought they could change the world. He read the Bible and challenged himself to come to understand its message and meaning.

He wrote "Suzanne" for his album "Songs of Leonard Cohen" (1967). The Suzanne was Suzanne Verdal, a dancer with whom Cohen had a platonic relationship. She would serve him Constant Comment tea and they would go for long walks together sometimes past the church of Notre-Dame-de-Bon-Secours, where sailors were blessed before heading out to sea. The song says:

> And Jesus was a sailor
> When he walked upon the water
> And he spent a long time watching
> From his lonely wooden tower.

Mary Martin had introduced Cohen to Judy Collins. Judy recorded his material and encouraged him to come on stage with her. It had seemed that Cohen was out of place in the new Folk scene. He was approaching his 33rd birthday.

Life in Hydra had been cheap and idyllic but it didn't pay the bills. So Cohen would return to Canada periodically. He met the dancer Suzanne Verdal. She became something of a muse for him. He read two poems for her; both were published in the 1966 Anthology "Parasites of Heaven". The two poems became the song "Suzanne". They never became lovers but were good friends. This explains the line about touching her perfect body with my mind.

On the church of Notre-Dame there is a statue of the Virgin Mary. She stands there with arms outstretched over the water, blessing the seafarers in the harbour. Cohen tells us that Jesus keeps a perpetual vigil in the wooden observation tower in the church. The lyrics of Suzanne are written on the walls of the tower.

The church is known as a sailor's church and seafarers still go there to pray. The church is full of model boats. This explains the line "and Jesus was a sailor when he walked upon the water." In the Gospels we see the miracle of Jesus walking on the water (Mk 6:54-53; Matthew 14:22-34; John 6:15-21). He knows that Jesus loves Suzanne as tenderly as he does. Cohen said:

> It was as though she handed me the seed for the song ... So Suzanne becomes an incarnation of that church for sailors, Notre-Dame-de-Bon-Secours or Our Lady of Consolation – that's her church. Suzanne becomes of course Our Lady of the Harbour, or she manifests as Our Lady of the Harbour ... Notre-Dame-de-Bon-Secours faces the river; the sailors are blessed from that church. So the next verse moves very easily to the idea that Jesus was a sailor.
>   (Harry Rasky, dir., The Songs of Leonard Cohen)

The sea will free people.

> And when he knew for certain
> Only drowning men could see him
> He said 'All men will be sailors then
> Until the sea shall free them.'

Freedman believed that Cohen was referring to an old Syrian legend. It tells the story of the apostle Andrew who rescues the apostle Matthew – Jesus steered the ship Andrew was on (Freedman, p. 106-108). Christianity had a spiritual attraction for Cohen. The songs and poems he wrote that he based on Jewish ideas tend to be philosophical, mystical or defiant, whereas his works inspired by Christianity, a simpler message of love and pety of spirit. He had a magic ability to draw out the best of every belief system he encountered and saw no conflict between them.

In a poem that Cohen wrote later he prays to Mary. He places himself under her care as the sailors did in the song Suzanne.

> You step out of the shower
> Oh so cool and clean
> Smelling like a flower
> From a field of green
> The world is burning Mary
> It's hollow dark and mean
>
> I love to hear you laugh
> It takes the world away
> I live to hear you laugh
> I don't even have to pray
> But now the world is coming back
> It's coming back to stay
>
> Stand beside me Mary
> We have no time to waste
> The water's not like water now
> It has a bitter taste
> Stand beside me Mary
> Mary full of grace

This poem was published in a posthumous collection of Cohen's poems called "The Flame".[8] His son, Adam, who wrote the foreword said that writing was his only solace, his only purpose (The Flame, p. 2). Writing brought him great relief unlike everything else he tried. It was there he was more completely himself. When Adam was a boy he would often

---

[8] Leonard Cohen, The Flame (Edinburgh: 2018).

find bits of paper where Cohen had jotted down lines of poetry. By the early 1990's there were storage boxes filled with notebooks. Writing was his reason for being. "It was the fire he was tending to, the most significant flame he fueled. It was never extinguished." His final album was "You Want It Darker" (2016). Cohen said "You want it darker, we kill the flame". Adam said in response "It feels darker now, but the flame was not killed. Each page of paper that he blackened was lasting evidence of a burning soul." (Flame, foreword).

Meditating with Leonard Cohen:
Leonard Cohen speaks to many because of his art, music, and poetry but also because people relate to his insights, knowing those insights were born of struggle. Laurent Cohen, a French writer, wrote a sort of meditation on Leonard Cohen's work.[9]

> Patience is our weapon,
> prayer our strategy,
> and sacrifice our understanding of the times.
> Take heart, you who have not been gathered yet,
> watch for the banner we have raised,
> and come to us when the walls
> of your sanctuary begin to give against the weight of tears.
> (The Flame, 231)

The poem shows the plight of the human being of flesh and blood before the infinite. This is part of the mystery that Cohen speaks of in his works. In Hebrew the word 'Cohen' means priest. Cohen believed he had received a heritage which shaped his place in the world.[10] Across the centuries the Cohen was the one who blessed and prayed for the people. The blessing of Moses to Aaron was the model for this: "The Lord bless you and keep you. May the Lord shine his face on you and be gracious to you. May the Lord turn his face towards you and give you peace" (Numbers 6:24-26). This is the prayer of the priest. The idea of this

---

[9] Laurent Cohen, Prier 15 jours avec Leonard Cohen: Poète mystique (Paris: 2023).
[10] Les Inrockuptibles, "Leonard Cohen, folk singer madame", no. 39, May 2009.

prayer penetrates Cohen's works. It echoes the prayer of the one who enters the Holy of Holies, the most interior part of the Temple in Jerusalem. He spoke of his cross:

> "But there will be a Cross, a sign, that some will understand; a secret meeting, a warning, a Jerusalem hidden in Jerusalem. I will be wearing white clothes, as usual, and I will enter The Innermost Place as I have done generation upon generation, to entreat, to plead, to justify. I will enter the chamber of the Bride and the Bridegroom, and no one will follow me.
>
> Have no doubt, in the near future we will be seeing and hearing much more of this sort of thing from people like myself."[11]

He prays from the abyss of loneliness and prays for those who are lonely. This thought permeates his work. He spoke of the need for retreat, solitude and silence. It is precisely there in ever changing darkness and light. This is the experience of the one who seeks God. He spoke of the loneliness of the quest.[12]

The souls seeking for God find themselves "surrounded and filled by the Name" (Book of Mercy, p. 50). The Name stands for the presence of God. Those who seek are always in the presence of the one they seek. This is the action of the Holy Spirit. "Prayer makes a ceremony for the words".[13] Even when the soul feels abandoned or unworthy our silence can become a prayer. We are never rejected by God even though we reject ourselves.

This mysticism of silence is rooted in the Bible. Ps 65:2 can be translated as "For you silence is a celebration". In 1 Kings 19:9-12 Elijah waits for God. God is not in the hurricane, nor in the fire but in what Cohen translates as the subtle voice of silence. God is present in the silence. We are not alone. Cohen says:

---

[11] Leonard Cohen, The Book of Longing (London: 2006), p. 36.
[12] Leonard Cohen, Book of Mercy (Edinburgh: 2019 edition), p. 20.
[13] Leonard Cohen, Selected Poems (London: 1994), p. 131.

If it is your will
that I say nothing more
and that my voice dissipate
I will cease to speak
Then I will wait to be called
If that is your will.
                 (From the album Various Positions, 1984)

Cohen places all his trust in the one to whom we pray in the silence and in the loneliness of our quest. "After having searched among the words, without ever finding respite, I went to you" (Book of Mercy, p. 14).

He spoke of the gifts God gave him. He wrote in 'Book of Mercy':

> "You let me sing, you lifted me up, you gave my soul a beam to travel on. You folded your distance back into my heart. You drew the tears back to my eyes. You hid me in the mountain of your word. You gave the injury a tongue to heal itself. You covered my head with my teacher's care, you bound my arm with my grandfather's strength. O beloved speaking, O comfort whispering in the terror, unspeakable explanation of the smoke and cruelty, undo the self-conspiracy, let me dare the boldness of joy."

We hear and see the tears and supplications rise from page to page. In spite of the darkness that surrounds the psalmist there is the certainty that grace and healing will come. David was seen as the herald of the Book of Psalms. In 'Les Inrockuptibles' he spoke about the influence of the Psalms and the writing of the Book of Mercy. He said the words of the psalms could only have come from someone whose back was to the wall. "I wished to reaffirm the tradition which I inherited, a certain way of speaking which comes from the Bible, from the Psalms, the Holy Readings. I wished to express my gratitude for having been heir to this tradition (p. 44). His album "Various Positions" in 1984 led to his "Book of Mercy" in 1985. "Speak to your child of his healing, in this place where we are for a moment" (Book of Mercy, p. 37). Though at times he doesn't believe he places his faith in God and places his doubt in the hands of God. He pleads:

> "Speak to me again. Speak to my words. Give this ghost the form of tears, that he move from nothing to sorrow, into Creation, even winter, even loss, that he have weight, that he be placed. Discover him in tears and make a place for his longing. Behold him in your court, one who upholds the throne of praises. Where have I been? I gave the world to the Accuser. Where do I go? I go to ask for pardon from the Most High."

In The Flame he prays for the healing of the Spirit. He finds he has the Spirit with him in his work.

> O gather up the brokenness
> And bring it to me now
> The fragrance of those promises
> You never dared to vow
> The splinters that you carry
> The cross you left behind
> Come healing of the body
> Come healing of the mind
>
> And let the heavens hear it
> The penitential hymn
> Come healing of the spirit
> Come healing of the limb
>
> Behold the gates of mercy
> In arbitrary space
> And none of us deserving
> The cruelty or the grace
>
> O solitude of longing
> Where love has been confined
> Come healing of the body
> Come healing of the mind

O see the darkness yielding
That tore the light apart
Come healing of the reason
Come healing of the heart

O troubled dust concealing
An undivided love
The Heart beneath is teaching
To the broken Heart above

O let the heavens falter
And let the earth proclaim:
Come healing of the Altar
Come healing of the Name

O longing of the branches
To lift the little bud
O longing of the arteries
To purify the blood

And let the heavens hear it
The penitential hymn
Come healing of the spirit
Come healing of the limb

And let the heavens hear it
The penitential hymn
Come healing of the spirit
Come healing of the limb
                (Flame, 118)

In the Book of Mercy he pleads for the Holy Spirit to come down to "this lonely place", and he asks him: "Return to the sorrow in which you have hidden your truth" (Book of Mercy, p. 28f). In a whimsical poem from the Book of Longing he speaks of the way the Spirit works in him.

> Pardon me, lords and ladies,
> if I do not think of myself as the disease.
> Pardon me if I receive the Holy Spirit
> without telling you about it.
> Pardon me,
> Commissars of the West,
> if you do not think
> I have suffered enough.
>
> (Book of Longing, p. 187)

The Spirit works in ways and people we do not expect. Cohen's struggles and surrender in faith help us in our struggles.

"Return to the Sorrow where you have hidden your truth".

Printed in Great Britain
by Amazon